WHEN THE BODY SPEAKS

Conflict, Illness, and the Quiet Work of Healing

Dr. Radar Onguetou

innovativeink
PUBLISHING
A Division of Kendall Hunt

Cover image Shutterstock.com

innovativeink
PUBLISHING
A Division of Kendall Hunt

www.innovativeinkpublishing.com
Send all inquiries to:
4050 Westmark Drive
Dubuque, IA 52004-1840

Print ISBN: 979-8-3197-2236-2
eBook ISBN: 979-8-3197-2237-9

Published in the United States of America

Contents

Dedication

To God first

For the breath that remained when I did not know how to ask for it.
For the mercy that held me when strength was no longer enough.
For the quiet faith that stayed when certainty fell away.
This book exists because You did not abandon me to survival alone.
You invited me into truth, presence, and return.

To Kristianna

My wife, my companion, my steady witness.
You saw the cost of my endurance well before I had words for it.
You stayed when I was still performing strength.
You stayed when silence felt safer than honesty.
You stayed when I did not yet know how to be present without proving myself.

Your patience was not passive. It was faithful.
Your love did not rush my healing or demand coherence before its time.

You taught me without sermon or pressure
that intimacy is built not by carrying everything alone,
but by remaining when things are unfinished.

This book carries your imprint in every place where I learned to slow down,
to listen, and to stay.

To Amarah

My daughter, my second beginning.
You did not arrive to complete a story.
You arrived to make illusion impossible.

In your presence I could no longer live abstractly or postpone truth.
You showed me that legacy is not what we leave behind.
It is how we live while someone is watching and trusting us.

You call me into a life that is gentler, truer, and more awake.
This book is part of my promise to you.
To listen early.
To live honestly.
To name what my body and soul are carrying.

This work is for both of you.
It was born from love, sustained by love, and returned to love.
With gratitude, humility, and hope.

Epigraph

"My flesh and my heart may fail,
but God is the strength of my heart
and my portion forever."

Psalm 73:26

Foreword

In May of 2020, Radar and I were both language teachers at a small boarding school tucked into an isolated rural town. The landscape was beautiful, but the environment was singular: predominantly white, often quiet, and occasionally suffocating. We were the only two Black male members of the teaching faculty. But we shared more than just that demographic distinction. He was an immigrant from Africa; I from the Caribbean. He had played NCAA Division 1 basketball; I was a Division 3 All American in track and field. Despite the roughly twenty-year gap in our ages, we recognized something in each other almost immediately—a familiar rhythm of experience, an unspoken understanding of what it meant to navigate certain spaces in certain bodies, and a shared, protective commitment to the students who watched us from the margins.

We spent long, necessary hours together that year. We hiked wooded trails that cut through the countryside, our conversations often acting as a form of decompression. We drove off campus in search of meals that tasted like home, or at least reminded us of it. We debated the trivial, but mostly we wrestled with the weighty: race, belonging, faith, masculinity, and the exhaustion of trying to lead well in an institution that often seemed to view us as symbolic rather than substantial. We talked often about the Black students on campus—how to protect their dignity while helping them find their voices in a place that seemed to want them to be seen but not heard.

Then, on May 25, 2020, George Floyd was killed in Minneapolis.

Against the already disorienting backdrop of the COVID-19 pandemic, the world seemed to tilt on its axis. I remember sitting in faculty Zoom meetings with my camera turned off, listening to colleagues discuss garden plans and summer travel, while I furiously refreshed news feeds. I felt a cocktail of despair, frustration at institutional inadequacy, and a deep, gnawing sense of impotence.

Off screen, Radar and I convened. We compared notes. We processed. We lamented. We strategized. I began attending protests off campus and invited him to join me. At first, he declined, citing his fiancée's legitimate concern for his safety. He was physically imposing—tall, broad-shouldered, built like a professional athlete—and in that rural setting, he was hyper-visible. His presence drew attention even in stillness. Eventually, however, he changed his mind, and we attended multiple protests together that summer.

At one gathering, what had been advertised as a community vigil quickly revealed itself to be a thinly veiled recruitment event for a political organization. We listened for a time, growing increasingly uncomfortable with the rhetoric. Then Radar had enough. He approached the organizers and asked for the microphone. For twenty minutes, he delivered a lucid, unscripted address—measured, incisive, morally grounded. Hundreds listened. When he finished, the applause was thunderous.

It was typical Radar. He commanded attention simply by entering a room. Brilliant by any measure, gifted at reading his audience, he turned even casual conversation into something memorable. When he spoke publicly, he held his listeners in a kind of death grip. People left feeling awed, unsettled, and inspired—as if something dormant within them had been called to attention. He was a force of nature, a pillar of performance and intellect.

In June of 2021, Radar left the boarding school we worked at together—one year after George Floyd's murder.

In June of 2023, I flew to Florida to watch him receive his doctorate. The room that day was filled with tall Black men—childhood friends and brothers who had come to celebrate one of their own. They sang. They danced. They beamed with pride. I stood among them, grateful to witness the culmination of his hard work and to honor a man who had stood beside me during one of the most pivotal seasons of my life.

And then, in July of 2023, came the call. He had suffered a stroke while overseas. Weeks after he returned, when we finally connected over FaceTime, I was unprepared for what I saw. Though I could see little more than his face, the change was undeniable. His speech—once fluid, commanding, rhythmic—was halting and slurred. At times his words were so soft they dissolved before reaching my ear. Our conversations felt foreign, and it took me many months before I felt I was again speaking to the man whose voice had once filled auditoriums and open fields.

The stroke was not merely a medical event. It was a total rupture.

This book emerges from that rupture. At its core lies Radar's central insight—what he calls his conflict–illness theory: the conviction that unresolved internal conflicts—emotional, relational, spiritual—do not remain politely contained within the psyche. They migrate. They surface. They inhabit the body. Illness, in this framing, is not random misfortune alone, but often the body's final, desperate articulation of truths the soul has long suppressed.

Whether one ultimately agrees with every contour of his theory is almost beside the point. What makes this book essential is the sheer, unvarnished courage with which he interrogates his own life. He does not use theory to distance himself from his vulnerability; he uses it to expose it.

The stroke becomes the turning point—not just because it is dramatic, though it is—but because it forces him to confront a lifelong pattern of performance, endurance, and self-erasure. The old identity—athlete, scholar, orator, high achiever, dependable pillar—had been constructed around strength and output. In many ways, it had served him well. It had earned admiration, opportunity, and influence. But it had also concealed deep fractures.

Recovery, as this memoir makes painfully clear, is not a linear ascent. It is a hidden war. It is relearning the mechanics of speech. It is confronting total dependency. It is sitting with the humiliation of limitations. It is negotiating the strain illness places on one's most intimate relationships. It is wrestling with faith when the God you trusted for protection allows your body to fail.

Radar does not romanticize this process. He writes of the tension between who he was and who he was becoming—between the man who could dominate a room and the man who now struggled to finish a sentence. He chronicles the grief of losing an identity that had once felt synonymous with his worth. Yet, from that grief emerges something sturdier than performance: coherence.

Perhaps the most transformative thread in this book is his discovery of unconditional belonging, crystallized through fatherhood. In holding his child, he encounters a belonging untethered to achievement. An infant does not applaud eloquence or demand endurance. An infant does not care about résumés. In that relationship, Radar confronts a radical truth: that worth need not be earned through exhaustion.

This shift reverberates outward—reshaping his understanding of leadership, partnership, faith, and friendship. Faith, once a tool for survival and perseverance, becomes a practice of presence and trust. Strength is redefined not as the suppression of limits, but as their honest acknowledgment. Leadership becomes less about commanding attention and more about alignment between the inner life and outward action.

For those facing their own health crises, this memoir offers solidarity and a lexicon for experiences often suffered in isolation. For caregivers, it reveals the complex emotional and relational terrain that illness rearranges. For educators and leaders, it challenges the culture of overextension that often masquerades as dedication. But perhaps most of all, this book is for anyone who has ever confused performance with belonging.

I have known Radar as a colleague, a protest companion, a scholar, and a friend. I have seen him command crowds and I have seen him struggle for syllables. I have watched him stand unflinching before injustice and tremble in the vulnerability of recovery. This book does not diminish the man I knew; it deepens him.

The same voice that once electrified a protest now invites you into a quieter revolution—one that begins not in the streets but within the self. It asks: Where are you divided? What conflicts have you buried? What might your body already be trying to tell you? And what would it mean to live not as an act of endurance, but as an act of alignment?

You are about to read a story of fracture, yes. But more than that, you are about to read a story of integration. Enter it slowly. Let it unsettle you. Let it question the myths you have inherited about strength and success. And when you finish, may you find yourself a little more honest, a little more coherent, and a little more free.

Preface

I did not begin this book with a publishing plan or a proposal. I began it with a hospital ceiling and the quiet sound of my own breath.

Until that moment, I would have described myself as disciplined, faithful, and steady. I carried responsibilities with seriousness. I entered rooms prepared. I believed that strength meant endurance and that love meant showing up without complaint. I believed that if I remained calm enough, thoughtful enough, prayerful enough, the storms around me would eventually settle. I believed that belonging was secured through composure.

My body disagreed.

The stroke did not interrupt a reckless life. It interrupted a committed one. I was not running from responsibility. I was living inside it. Yet something in me had been absorbing more than it could metabolize. Conversations left unfinished. Disappointments named politely but not processed. Moments when I chose harmony over honesty. Each decision seemed small at the time. None of them felt dramatic. Together, they accumulated.

In the hospital I discovered that the body keeps an honest record. It remembers what the mind reframes and what the spirit postpones. It speaks when language has been overmanaged. Lying there, unable to rely on my usual composure, I saw how much of my life had been organized around being reliable rather than being whole.

This book emerges from that realization.

I write as a scholar trained to study conflict, belonging, and organizational life. I have spent years helping students and colleagues name tensions that hide beneath polite surfaces. I have taught that unresolved conflict does not disappear. It relocates. I believed that insight. I had not yet applied it fully to myself.

What I came to understand through illness is simple and difficult. Conflict that is not acknowledged within will eventually express itself somewhere. In my story, it expressed itself in my body. This is not a medical claim. It is a lived observation. The body became the place where accumulated strain refused further negotiation.

Recovery required more than physical therapy. It required moral clarity. I had to examine how I defined faithfulness, how I understood leadership, and how I negotiated belonging. I had to admit that some of what I called humility was avoidance. Some of what I called resilience was fear of disappointing others. Some of what I called peace was silence purchased at my own expense.

Healing did not restore an earlier version of me. It reordered me.

Kristianna stood beside me when my confidence thinned. She did not rush my healing or dramatize my fragility. She steadied it. Our daughter Amarah arrived not as a symbolic answer to suffering but as a daily reminder that love does not require performance. Holding her, I began to feel a form of belonging that was not conditional on output or composure. That experience reshaped how I think about leadership, marriage, faith, and vocation.

This book follows that reshaping.

Part I returns to the years when everything appeared strong while strain accumulated quietly. Part II enters the interior and relational work of recovery, where identity wavers and roles must be renegotiated. Part III traces a second beginning, where coherence replaces urgency and vocation is lived without exporting its cost onto the body or onto others.

I do not write as someone who has mastered these lessons. I write as someone practicing them. I still notice the impulse to carry too much. I still feel the temptation to secure belonging through overextension. What has changed is that I no longer ignore the signals. I pause. I listen. I speak sooner.

If you are reading these pages, you may not share my exact story. You may never experience a stroke. Yet you may recognize the fatigue of constant composure or the strain of being the stabilizing presence in every room. You may know what it feels like to manage conflict externally while suppressing it internally. You may sense that your body reacts when your heart remains unheard.

This book does not offer a formula. It offers an account. It is a reflection shaped by faith, scholarship, and lived experience. It invites careful attention to the relationship between conflict, belonging, and embodiment. It asks whether endurance alone is a sufficient measure of maturity. It proposes that coherence is more faithful than performance.

I begin with the body because that is where my truth became unavoidable. I continue with language because naming what has been carried is a form of release. If these pages help you notice your own patterns sooner than I noticed mine, then this work has done its part.

Let us begin with honesty and with the humility to listen before the body is forced to speak.

Author's Note

This book carries real names, real places, and real seasons of my life. It also carries restraint.

What you will read here is faithful to what I lived, but it is not exhaustive. Some conversations have been shortened. Some identifying details have been adjusted. Certain moments are compressed in order to protect the dignity of those who walked through them with me. The heart of each event remains intact. The private lives of others remain their own.

I write as someone formed by both scholarship and story. I have spent years studying conflict, belonging, leadership, and organizational life. I have taught that unresolved tension rarely disappears on its own. It relocates. It seeks a container. For a long time I understood that pattern professionally. Illness forced me to understand it personally.

The reflections in these pages grow from lived experience rather than controlled experiment. They are not medical conclusions. They are observations shaped by embodiment, prayer, and professional practice. Where I speak of conflict living in the body, I do so as a man describing his own history. I do not reduce illness to a single cause. I resist simple explanations. The body is complex. Suffering is layered. Meaning is never mechanical.

You will notice that this book moves between the personal and the institutional. That movement is intentional. I live in classrooms, dormitories, conference rooms, and hallways where young people and adults try to make sense of belonging. The dynamics I describe are not abstract to me. They are daily realities. The tensions of race, identity, power, expectation, and faith do not remain theoretical when you accompany students and colleagues through them. They become relational and embodied.

If you are looking for a manual, you will not find one here. If you are looking for a testimony without complication, this is not that either. What I offer is an account of fracture and coherence. An account of how silence can feel virtuous while slowly extracting a cost. An account of how faith matures when it is no longer used to outrun limits. An account of how leadership must be reimagined when the body refuses to carry what a system will not hold.

My wife, Kristianna, read early drafts of this manuscript. At times she would remind me that the most important changes in my life did not happen in public. They happened in kitchens, in hospital rooms, in conversations when my voice was uncertain. My daughter, Amarah, will one day read these pages. I want her to know that her father did not wait for collapse to tell the truth. I want her to inherit a home where limits are honored and belonging is not purchased with disappearance.

This book is not written from a place of arrival. I continue to learn. I still feel the impulse to overextend. I still recognize the temptation to secure approval through competence. What has changed is not that I no longer struggle. It is that I no longer pretend struggle has no cost.

If you find yourself in these pages, I hope you encounter not instruction but companionship. I hope you feel permitted to examine your own patterns without shame. I hope you notice the signals your body offers before crisis amplifies them. And I hope you discover, as I did, that belonging grounded in truth is steadier than belonging secured through silence.

Thank you for reading with patience and with care.

Prologue

I begin where the book truly begins, with my body.

Not the body as metaphor, not the body as medical object, but the living body that carried my work, my faith, my ambition, my responsibilities, and my silence. The body that kept pace with my intentions long after my heart had grown tired of performing strength.

For years I lived at a fast rhythm. I worked hard, prayed hard, and carried many responsibilities without complaint. I believed that if I stayed calm, faithful, and composed, my body would follow. I treated peace as restraint and conflict as something to manage rather than name. I learned too late that what is not spoken does not disappear. It travels inward and settles in the body.

The stroke did not arrive as a lesson I sought. It came as an interruption that rearranged my life. In that hospital bed I saw how fragile my control had been and how much I had been absorbing quietly. My body spoke in a language I could no longer ignore. It remembered what I had refused to face and revealed truths I had postponed too long.

In that stillness I began to see something I had missed for years. I had treated belonging as something to earn through quiet sacrifice, by absorbing tension, carrying more than I should, and keeping the peace even when it wounded me. I believed this was faithfulness. Lying there, I realized how gently and painfully I had been wrong. True belonging does not ask the body to disappear or the heart to go silent. It invites truth, limits, and presence. My body stopped me not to shame me, but to teach me that I could be loved, held, and accepted without paying for it with my own erasure.

This book was born in that rupture, not in pride, but in humility and trembling gratitude for still being here.

Recovery did not move in a straight line. It unfolded in quiet rooms, sleepless nights, slow walks, and prayers spoken with tears. It unfolded in honest conversations with Kristianna that changed me, and later in the fragile joy of holding my daughter Amarah. Healing was not restoration. It was alignment — a slow learning to live in a way that would not require my body to speak in crisis to be heard.

Alignment, I discovered, is quieter than ambition and far more demanding.

Out of this experience emerged what I now call the conflict illness framework. I did not invent it in an office. I discovered it in my own flesh. Conflict that remains unnamed — internal, relational, or organizational — does not vanish. When it becomes too heavy to carry silently, the body becomes its messenger. Illness, in my story, was not punishment or accident. It was interruption, a truthful mediation that made visible what had been unsustainable.

This book moves slowly on purpose. I resist tidy arcs of before, crisis, recovery, after because they flatten what actually happened. Life does not resolve neatly. Healing unsettles identity before it clarifies it. Presence must be relearned, and limits must become teachers rather than threats.

The book unfolds in three movements, not stages to complete, but inner orientations.

Part I returns to the life before fracture, where everything appeared strong while strain quietly accumulated. Nothing was broken yet. Everything was already under pressure.

Part II enters the hidden war of recovery, where the body no longer negotiates, relationships must reorganize, and silence becomes exposure rather than protection. Here disorientation is not hurried, because truth takes time to arrive.

Part III marks a shift toward coherence, not closure. Survival loosens its grip. Faith becomes practice rather than explanation. Vocation is lived without exporting its cost onto the body or onto others. This is where a second beginning takes root — life continuing without erasing what came before, shaped by memory rather than governed by fear.

You may not have had a stroke, but you may recognize the weight of carrying too much, the cost of keeping peace at your own expense, or the fatigue of constant resilience. If so, this book is for you as much as it is for me.

I do not offer a model to master. I invite you to notice patterns. Where effort replaces truth. Where belonging is negotiated through erasure. Where silence accumulates until it becomes somatic. Notice, before crisis insists.

I write as a man still healing, still learning, still being reshaped. A husband carried by love when I could not stand alone. A father called into a gentler, truer way of living. A scholar who now believes that insight is trustworthy only when it has passed through lived experience.

This book does not close a story. It offers a posture that can be inhabited after fracture, without denial, without haste, and without betraying what has been revealed.

Let us walk this path together, slowly, human to human.

PART I

WHEN LIFE FRACTURES

1

WHEN LIFE BREAKS THE RHYTHM

I did not begin this story with a diagnosis.

I began it with a rhythm.

Long before the stroke, my life was not a sequence of visible catastrophes. It was a sequence of yeses, responsibilities accepted, opportunities taken, doors opened that I felt I must never close again. I was convinced that this was what faithfulness looked like: keep moving, keep working, honor the sacrifices of others, show God that I was doing my part.

I called it perseverance.

Looking back, I can see that sometimes it was also an escape.

This first chapter goes back before the machines, the scans, the IV drips. It tells the season when everything still stood upright on the outside, while inside, a crack was already forming.

Long before the body collapses, silent conflicts accumulate. They settle into choices, pace, loyalties, the way we love, and the way we allow ourselves to be loved. They do not speak right away. They take their time. Then, one day, they look for a language stronger than our explanations.

In Chapter 1, life breaks the rhythm. In Chapter 2, the body, tired of carrying alone, becomes the messenger.

SECTION I — THE CRACKING RHYTHM

Life does not always fall apart all at once. Most of the time, it settles in.

You wake up, you follow your schedule, you do what needs to be done. One day slips into the next. Months become years. At some point, you no longer ask whether the rhythm is good for you. You only ask:

"Am I still holding up?"

For a long time, that was my life.

I was a son and a brother.

I was a child of Yaoundé who became "the African in America."

I was a basketball player, a student, then a teacher, a coach, a doctoral student, and eventually a Director of Community Engagement, Diversity and Belonging.

I carried all those roles with pride, and with a stubborn determination that left almost no room for rest, for questions, or for limits.

I did not ask myself, "Does this pace honor God, my body, my family?"

I asked only, "Am I still managing to stand?"

Looking back, I can see that I was already living inside a quiet conflict between what I showed the world and what my body and my soul were trying to tell me before God.

Today I have a professional language for it: intrapsychic conflict, the internal tension between identity, loyalties, fears, and beliefs that, when ignored for too long, eventually looks for another language.

For me, that language became the body.

What we refuse to face within ourselves often finds another way to speak.

In my case, that truth took a brutal name: stroke.

But the stroke does not tell the whole story. It is not the beginning. It is the visible fracture of an inner structure that had been cracking for years.

To understand what happened on July 11, 2023, in Yaoundé, I have to go back to the beginning, not as if I were reciting a résumé, but as if I were rereading a story of loyalties, silences, pressures, and repeated choices. It is a story in which, very early on, I learned to replace emotion with action and need with performance, believing sincerely that this was the best way not to dishonor those who were praying for me.

SECTION II — LEAVING YAOUNDÉ

August 2004.

I leave Yaoundé with a suitcase, a dream, and one sentence looping in my head:

"You must not fail."

I do not yet have the vocabulary for migration trajectory, symbolic pressure, or intrapsychic conflict. I only know this:

My parents sacrificed a lot.

God opened a door.

I do not have the right to close it through failure.

I leave Cameroon carried by the prayers of my mother and father. They entrust me to God the way you place a child into the hands of Someone greater. I leave behind the heat of Yaoundé, the house in Essos, the voices, the smells, the laughter, the familiar, living, breathing chaos of home.

I arrive in the United States on a student visa with a strong accent, a basketball player's body, and a scholarship to play at New Hampton School in New Hampshire.

From August 2004 to May 2006, my life is paced by classes, homework, essays in a language that is not the one I grew up in, practices, the weight room, games, the pressure to perform, and a constant inner vigilance:

"Show them they were not wrong to believe in you.

Do not disappoint God who opened this path for you."

I meet my American host family. They open their house, their refrigerator, their traditions. I owe them a great deal.

But even inside that home, full of goodwill, I remain inwardly between two worlds.

I remember my first winter. The cold cut your face. Night fell early. After practice I went up to my room on campus. Others went back to their biological families. I was housed, surrounded, and yet profoundly displaced.

Christmas and New Year's Eve were especially painful.

Everyone seemed happy. I carried in my body the absence of the warmth of Yaoundé, the loud conversations, family meals, church services, the songs, the jokes, the smells, and the chaos of holiday gatherings back home.

My host family did not understand my quiet withdrawal. One day they held a family meeting to tell me I did not have the holiday spirit, that I seemed closed off and distant.

I felt misunderstood, almost guilty, as if my sadness betrayed their generosity.

I promised to try harder.

But it was not a lack of effort.

It was the pain of separation.

I did not have the words for it. I did not want to worry my parents on the phone. I did not want to be a problem for the people hosting me.

So I began to do something that would mark my entire trajectory: I buried my emotions and replaced them with action.

I told myself that this was strength. That crying, naming loneliness, admitting homesickness were negative emotions I needed to eliminate. Over time, I started to believe those emotions were gone.

They were simply moving deeper, into a place I did not dare show to others, to God, or to myself.

That is where a quiet link was already forming between inner conflict and the body.

I did not get sick then, but my body was storing the sleepless nights, the tension, the held back tears, the invisible pressure.

It kept everything in memory.

SECTION III — LIFE IN LAYERS

By the time I arrived at the University of New Hampshire, the rhythm I had learned to accept was no longer temporary. It was becoming a way of life.

In May 2006, I finished New Hampton and enrolled at the University of New Hampshire. That same summer, I joined the university basketball team.

From 2006 to 2011, my life became layered, almost stacked, one obligation on top of another, with no real space in between.

I am a full-time student.

I am a college athlete.

I am also a worker.

As a student, I read, write, attend classes, and try to grasp concepts in a language that still feels new. I sit in lecture halls taking notes, translating ideas in my head before I can even begin to think critically about them.

As an athlete, my days are shaped by practice schedules, weight room sessions, games, travel, and recovery. My strength builds. I reach a goal of bench pressing 500 pounds. My body is expected to perform, to stay strong, to stay reliable.

As a worker, I do what is necessary to survive. I need to cover my expenses. I need to send some money back home. I need to make sure I am not a burden to anyone.

Concretely, this means early mornings receiving food deliveries in the campus cold room, working the hot line in the cafeteria, sometimes at the omelet station, sometimes at the wok, wiping tables, cleaning floors while other students are heading out, and in the evenings, several times a week, checking IDs as a bouncer at a bar in town. In between all of that, I am writing papers, studying for exams, sitting in class, trying not to fall asleep.

The days are full.

The mind is full.

The body is constantly solicited.

In May 2009, I earned my bachelor's degree.

In May 2011, I completed my master's degree at UNH.

On the graduation photos, there is a smile, a gown, a sense of achievement. What does not show is the inner conviction that is slowly solidifying:

The more I do, the more I exist.

The more I produce, the more I earn the right to be here.

Without ever stating it this way, I am also learning the role of the good immigrant.

No one spells it out, but you feel it.

Be grateful.

Do not complain.

Do not take up too much space.

Do not fail.

Make your family proud.

Justify the opportunity you were given.

I understand very quickly that I am not perceived only as Radar. I am also "the Cameroonian," "the African," "the scholarship athlete." I am carrying something larger than myself, whether I want to or not.

This creates a deep internal tension: being myself and at the same time representing something for others.

At that point, I still believe my body will keep up. I am young. I am athletic. I am strong. I do not see that I am already normalizing a level of overexertion that will later demand payment.

I also do not see that this rhythm will eventually collide with the limits God placed in my body, not to restrict me, but to protect me.

SECTION IV — LEARNING TO CARRY

By 2011, the student years had formed something in me. Not just discipline, but a habit of carrying without interruption.

In 2011, I returned to New Hampton School, this time as a teacher.

I crossed to the other side.

I became the one who sets the frame, who teaches, who supervises, who holds responsibility. I took this role seriously, perhaps too seriously.

In my mind, being a good adult, a good role model, meant being solid, available, dependable, and discreet about personal struggles.

I stayed in the same internal script:

"You must show that you deserve your place.

You must prove that you are worthy of everything that was invested in you."

I did not yet see the cost of that script.

I did not see how much my identity was beginning to collapse into my performance. I was proud to be a teacher. I was proud to work in an environment that values rigor and excellence. But I began, without naming it, to learn something that would take me years to articulate:

When your identity becomes too tightly bound to what you do, any weakness in what you do threatens everything you believe you are.

A quiet conflict settled in between the man I was and the role I believed I had to play in order to remain legitimate.

Somewhere in the middle of that tension, the voice of God became quieter, not absent, but increasingly covered by the noise of obligations, expectations, and self-imposed pressure.

At the time, I still interpreted this silence as maturity, as discipline, as growth. I did not recognize it yet as the early signs of disconnection from myself, from my body, and eventually from the kind of rest God intends.

SECTION V — FLORIDA AND KRISTIANNA

What began as responsibility in New Hampshire deepened in Florida. The pace intensified, but so did the possibility of love.

August 2016.

I leave New England and move to Florida. I begin a doctoral program in conflict analysis and resolution at Nova Southeastern University. At the same time, I take a teaching position at Monarch High School in Coconut Creek.

I move back in with my host family, who once again open their home to me. Their generosity continues to hold me, even as my life becomes more demanding.

That year, I met Kristianna.

I remember the first time I truly noticed her.

There was nothing theatrical about it. No spotlight. No slowed moment. It was quieter than that, almost sacred. She stepped into the room with an unforced presence, as if she was not trying to take up space and yet somehow illuminated it. At first, it was not her smile that unsettled me. It was her face, striking in its natural beauty, a slender, tall frame, almost 5'10", with a grace that felt both elegant and unassuming. And her lips, beautiful in a way I do not think I ever told her. They were the kind of detail you notice once and never forget.

Her style only added to the impression. She wore white pants with a dress shirt, or sometimes a long, elegant skirt, something rare to see where we were. She carried herself with ease, refined without effort, confident without noise. She was, in every sense, stylish.

Her long, dark, softly curly hair softened her presence even more. And when she leaned in to speak, I caught the faintest trace of her perfume, light, clean, almost floral. It stayed with me longer than the conversation itself. Even now, I can recall the way something in me loosened when I heard her laugh. Not the polite laugh people offer in public settings, but the real one, the kind that escapes before someone has time to manage their image.

Yet beauty was only part of it. What struck me most was the peace around her, a steadiness I did not know I needed. She acted as though she was not impressed by all my movement, all my striving. Her gentleness had weight. It met my restlessness without flinching, and still, somewhere beneath that calm, I sensed she was interested too.

Looking back, I think God was already writing the story before I had the courage to read it. I noticed her because, for the first time in a long time, something in my spirit recognized a place to breathe.

I met Kristianna between August and September 2016. We started dating shortly after. There was ease between us, depth, curiosity. I fell in love with her quickly, and sincerely.

On paper, everything looked aligned:

A doctorate in a field that made sense to me.

A teaching position.

A relationship that felt promising and alive.

But the daily reality I built was almost inhuman.

A typical day looked like this:

In the morning, I was fully present at Monarch, teaching, listening to students, managing classrooms, responding to needs that did not wait.

In the afternoon, there was coaching, supervision, and meetings.

At the end of the day, I got in the car and drove to Davie for evening doctoral seminars at Nova.

At night, I returned late, graded assignments, read academic articles, responded to emails, worked on research papers.

And then I woke up and did it again.

In the middle of all this, I tried to be a present partner to Kristianna. We built our relationship in hallways, in car rides, in brief moments between obligations. We talked deeply, but often while moving, while transitioning, while already thinking about what came next. And yet, even in those rushed fragments of time, something about her slowed me down. She had a way of turning a parking lot into a conversation room, a five-minute walk into a place of honesty. Sometimes she tilted her head slightly when she listened, as if to make more room for what I was trying to say. Other times, she smiled in that quiet, knowing way of hers, the kind of smile that made my shoulders drop without me realizing it.

There were evenings when we stayed in the car long after we arrived. The engine was off. The world outside was quiet. We talked about our childhoods, our fears, and the fragile hopes we carried for a life we were still learning how to build.

It was in those conversations that she shared her story. Kristianna is Armenian and Persian. As refugees, she and her mother fled to Germany, where she grew up. I immediately recognized something familiar. We both understood the quiet expectations placed on immigrants. Be grateful. Do not complain. Do not sound unthankful. And beneath all of it lives the same feeling that, no matter how well you adapt, you may never fully belong.

That recognition drew us closer. Her presence slowed my urgency. She asked questions that made me feel seen, and she answered mine with an honesty that still surprises me. Even in the busiest seasons of my life, she created small spaces where my spirit could finally breathe.

But the truth is that I did not ask her the kind of questions she longed for, the personal ones that would have shown her that I was genuinely curious about who she was beneath the surface. She told me, more than once, that it made her wonder whether I was truly interested in knowing her. And she was right. I rarely went in depth. Conversations with me could feel like pulling teeth. I held my inner world too tightly, spoke little about myself, and often hid behind silence or efficiency.

Still, she tried. Repeatedly, she reached for connection, not out of pressure or performance, but out of love. A steady, patient love. The kind that keeps showing up even when the other person does not know how to open the door.

During the doctorate, success took on a very specific meaning in my mind: not failing.

I had seen too many people begin PhD programs and never finish. I repeated to myself:

"That will not be me."

To succeed meant completing the program, earning the degree within a reasonable time, proving that my parents' sacrifices were not in vain, showing that a child from Cameroon could hold his own in these spaces.

Success also meant having something in my hands that could not be taken away, a title, a credential, a form of recognition no one could dispute.

And behind all of this, even if I rarely said it out loud, there was fear: I could not disappoint anyone.

Not my family back home.

Not my host family.

Not the professors who believed in me.

Not the woman I was building a life with.

Not God, whom I asked to bless this race, without always asking whether the race itself was healthy.

Achievement became armor.

It proved that I belonged.

It justified my exhaustion.

It covered my depletion.

But it also prevented me from saying, "I am not okay. I need help."

SECTION VI — LIVING TOGETHER

Love deepened, but my way of living did not. When we moved under the same roof, I brought the same pace with me.

In January 2017, I left my host family's house for good. I moved in with Kristianna. We created a home together.

It was an important step. A commitment. A beginning.

But I entered that home with the same internal logic:

A saturated calendar.

A crowded mind.

A body pushed beyond its limits.

A heart that stayed mostly silent.

My inner voice during those years was firm, almost harsh:

"Keep going. Do not slow down.

You do not have the right to be tired.

Do not complain.

Rise above certain things.

You are better than this."

I gave myself no margin for error.

No space for vulnerability.

No permission to say, "I cannot do this anymore."

When things became difficult, I told myself, "That is just life. Stay focused. Find a way."

And when I reached my limits, I turned to God, but often in the form of negotiation:

"Lord, if You give me the strength to keep going, I promise I will..."

My faith remained real, but it gradually shifted into survival mode. God became the One I asked to help me continue, not the One who was allowed to tell me, "Stop. Rest. Change."

In our early relationship, and in the years that followed, cracks began to appear. Not loud arguments. Often something more difficult to name: silence. The kind of silence that does not erupt but settles. A silence shaped less by anger than by exhaustion, by two people trying to hold on while life pulled them in too many directions. A silence that revealed gaps we did not yet have the tools or the courage to bridge.

Kristianna spoke.

I was physically present, but mentally elsewhere.

I said "I'm fine" out of reflex. I did not show her the dangerous fatigue that was accumulating.

What I would have needed from her was not only romantic love, but a gentleness that says, "You can take off your armor here."

I did not know how to ask for that. I thought it would make me a burden.

Sometimes I told her, "Please speak gently to me. I do not respond well when voices are raised." But even when she spoke gently, I remained closed.

I did not give her access to my fears, my insecurities, my doubts. I wanted to be the rock. I did not want to worry her.

The result was that I deprived her of the chance to be a true partner. And I deprived myself of the chance to be truly known, by her and by God working through this marriage.

This refusal to let myself be fully seen was another form of inner conflict.

And I kept it tightly held.

My body, meanwhile, continued to take notes.

SECTION VII — LOVE ACROSS BORDERS

The more our commitment deepened, the more life tested it. Love remained, but so did distance, paperwork, and strain.

In August 2017, I asked Kristianna to marry me. She said yes.

It was a moment of joy, of relief, of hope. But our story did not move forward in a straight line. Love did not cancel fatigue. Commitment did not erase unspoken tensions.

There were misunderstandings. Moments when my emotional distance, my exhaustion, my habit of carrying everything alone created gaps between us. We separated. We reconciled. We tried again.

In 2018, another layer of complexity was added: Kristianna had to return to Germany, to Düsseldorf, to renew her visa.

She left.

The visa was denied.

Another separation.

Another distance imposed by paperwork.

Another relationship forced to live through screens, messages, and time zones.

We broke up again.

We came back together again.

Nothing was simple, neither in our hearts nor on official documents.

In the middle of all this, I continued my doctorate, my job, my pace. I did not adapt anything to my fatigue. I did not slow down. I did not reconfigure my life around the fragility of our relationship.

I asked God to make it work, without asking myself how I might collaborate with that grace by changing my way of living.

The strain deepened. I kept asking my body to support emotional uncertainty, relational strain, and relentless productivity all at once.

SECTION VIII — MARRIAGE AND DISTANCE

By the fall of 2018, major milestones arrived. From the outside, they looked like resolution. Inside, the strain continued.

On September 28, 2018, I became a U.S. citizen.

It was a powerful moment. The child who left Yaoundé in 2004 officially became a citizen of a country where he had long lived as a guest.

Less than a month later, on October 27, 2018, Kristianna and I got married at Lake Louise, near Calgary, where my sister lives.

The setting was breathtaking. The moment was unforgettable. The celebration carried much of our story within it: movement, diaspora, extended family, the decision to unite despite borders.

We said yes to each other away from both of our homes. On October 27, 2018, at Lake Louise, surrounded by mountains and cold air that felt almost ceremonial, we made a promise that carried both of our journeys, movement, diaspora, hope, and a desire for something steady. It was a beautiful beginning, but like most beginnings, it happened in the middle of everything else: distance, deadlines, unfinished studies, and the weight of lives still unfolding on different continents.

At the end of 2018, I flew to Germany, to Düsseldorf, to spend time with Kristianna and to meet her mother. I came to love her mother as if she were my own, warm, gracious, attentive in the way that makes you feel welcomed long before you sit down. Kristianna and I traveled together to Paris. We walked. We talked. We tried to build something stable across distance, trying to make a home out of days that were already numbered.

But even in those tender moments, the reality of immigration hung over us. Marriage did not mean she could simply come home with me. After the wedding, she returned to Germany while we began the long, procedural journey of applying for her residency. Anyone looking from a distance might think the story was resolved. You are married now, so you can finally be together. But that is not how the process works. Paperwork, interviews, security checks, government timelines, months of silence. A system that moves at its own pace, unaffected by love, fear, or longing. We loved each other, and yet we still had to part again. It is a strange kind of ache: being united in covenant while still divided by borders.

I flew back to the United States with that ache sitting quietly in my chest. It was a heaviness I carried alone, because I did not yet know how to name the emotional cost of a life lived in fragments. I returned to my work, my studies, my commitments. I told myself we would be okay, that God would make a way, that love was enough to fill the distance. But beneath that faith, another truth was forming: the pace of my life left almost no room for the tenderness that love requires. I kept moving. I kept producing. I kept living as if rest and presence were luxuries I had not earned.

As 2019 began, the geography of our relationship continued to expand: Germany, the Dominican Republic, Morocco, Italy, Toronto, places filled with beauty, memory, and the relief of reunion. And yet, even as the world opened to us, the pace tightened around me. Travel became both joy and burden. The suitcase that never fully emptied became a mirror of my inner life: always in motion, rarely at rest, held together by the momentum of expectations.

The tension grew quietly. I wanted to be a good husband. I wanted to be a good son, a good teacher, a good doctoral candidate, a good immigrant. But the more I tried to hold everything, the less of myself I had available to offer. The conflict deepened: the desire to be present everywhere, and the impossibility of being whole anywhere.

This is the threshold that leads into 2019, a year filled with movement, celebration, and deepening fatigue. A year when the distance began to close geographically, but the cracks within me began to widen.

SECTION IX — THE GEOGRAPHY OF DISTANCE

In 2019, love and travel filled the calendar. So did parting. Every reunion carried beauty, and every goodbye left a mark.

In March 2019, Kristianna and I met in the Dominican Republic. Santo Domingo. Punta Cana. We celebrated her birthday on the 27th, with the sea as a witness.

That same year, we officially submitted her green card application. We wanted, finally, to live in the same place, without administrative borders between us.

In June 2019, I flew to Mainz, Germany. We spent time together there, then traveled to Morocco. It became one of our most beautiful journeys: colors, scents, long conversations, the unfamiliar that draws you closer. We returned to Mainz, then left again in July for Italy.

Each place we visited that year carried its own beauty. The colors of Morocco, the quiet mornings in Mainz, the evenings in Rome when we walked side by side without knowing when life would allow us to walk like that again. Travel had its wonders, but beneath the photographs and the laughter, something quieter lived in both of us, the awareness that every reunion carried its own expiration date. Love was present, steady, growing, but always accompanied by the shadow of another goodbye.

Each place carried beauty.

Each reunion carried relief.

Each departure carried its own quiet grief.

And some goodbyes have carved themselves into my memory with a clarity I still feel in my chest.

Santo Domingo and Punta Cana carried the same rhythm, joy, fullness, and then the slow, painful countdown. We timed our flights so we would at least drive to the same airport, even if our terminals were different. I always acted as though I was ready to leave, as if the transition back to my responsibilities came naturally. The reality was different. I dreaded the last day so much that pretending became easier than admitting how much it hurt. She knew it too. She could see beneath the performance. At the airport curb, she held onto me a little longer than usual, her head resting against my chest. I inhaled the scent of her hair, trying to store it somewhere deep enough to last the months ahead. When we finally pulled apart, she wiped her tears quickly, and I turned away before she could see mine. I felt devastated but hid it because I did not yet know how to carry both love and vulnerability at the same time.

In every place, Frankfurt, Santo Domingo, Punta Cana, the pattern was the same. We soaked up every moment, trying to stretch minutes into something that could hold us until the next reunion. I often walked toward security with the posture of someone who had made peace with distance. Inside, I was anything but peaceful. Each goodbye felt like tearing a fabric that had only just begun to mend.

In Germany, she accompanied me to Frankfurt Airport. That entire journey, Germany to Morocco, back to Germany, then to Italy, back again, and finally to the United States, felt like one long attempt to outrun another goodbye. She carried my bag with me through the terminal, not because I needed help, but because neither of us wanted to let go of the small, ordinary ways we took care of each other. We walked slowly, as if time might show mercy if we did not rush it.

At the departure hall, she stood close to me, her arm brushing mine with every small movement. I kept telling her I would be fine, that I was ready, that I needed to get back to work. None of that was true. I was trying to convince myself, not her. When they called for boarding, she tightened her grip on my hand as if she could hold the moment still. Her eyes glistened, but she tried to keep them steady. I felt my own begin to burn.

We hugged, long and quiet, both of us breathing in the same slow rhythm, as if memorizing each other might soften the ache that was coming. For a few seconds, I let my forehead rest against hers. I whispered that I loved her, and she nodded the way she does when words are too fragile to carry everything she feels.

When I finally turned toward security, I felt her watching me. I looked back once more, and she lifted her hand. Not waving. Just holding it there, suspended between blessing and longing. I carried that image with me onto the plane, into the clouds, into the next season of miles and months apart.

Long distance love is not measured in geography alone. It is measured in how much of your heart you leave behind at every airport. And on that day, leaving Frankfurt, I felt the weight of it in my chest, a quiet grief, a quiet devotion, and a hope that one day the departures would end, and the arrivals would no longer have a countdown.

What I did not realize then was how much that rhythm, of loving deeply while living divided, was shaping the inner tension that would follow me into the next years. Distance does not simply separate bodies. It stretches the soul. And stretching, when unexamined, eventually tears. Even as our love grew stronger, my life did not slow down, my responsibilities did not loosen, and my body, already carrying more than I would admit, continued to absorb what my heart refused to name.

In August 2019, I accepted a position at Cushing Academy and moved to Ashburnham, Massachusetts. In October, we met in Toronto to celebrate our first wedding anniversary. In December, I flew back to Düsseldorf to spend the holidays with Kristianna and her mother.

From the outside, this life can look enviable: travel, love, projects, smiling photos. From the inside, it is also made of suitcases that are never fully unpacked, bodies that never fully rest, a heart stretched across continents, a calendar that leaves no empty spaces, and professional demands that never loosen their grip.

I wanted to be a good husband, a good teacher, a good doctoral candidate, a good son, a good immigrant. I left myself very little room to simply be a man who was allowed to be tired, a man loved by God even when he was not checking every box.

The inner conflict grew: the desire to be present everywhere, and the impossibility of being whole anywhere.

SECTION X — PANDEMIC AND PRESSURE

Then the world stopped moving, at least outwardly. But inwardly, the strain only changed form.

In March 2020, another plan collapsed.

A reunion was scheduled. The trip was canceled. Covid spread. Borders closed. Campuses emptied. Classes moved online.

For the first time in a long while, the external world was forced to slow down.

Physically, my pace eased for a few weeks. There was less travel. Fewer meetings. Fewer miles driven.

But inside, something else stirred.

The summer of 2020 was marked by the murder of George Floyd and the Black Lives Matter protests. I watched the images as a Black man, an immigrant, an educator, a coach, a husband, a believer.

The footage, the chants, the marches awakened things I had buried: the suspicious looks I had learned to read, the feeling of being accepted only within certain limits, the pressure of having to represent well.

I think back to a trip in 2012, at the central market in Yaoundé, when vendors called me "the American" and raised their prices. I told them, "I'm from here." They smiled, unconvinced.

It hurts to realize that I do not fully belong anywhere: here, my accent, my skin, my origin marks me as different. There, my departure, my absence, my new habits do the same.

The role of the good immigrant weighs heavily. No one hands you a script, but you learn it quickly: be perfect, be grateful, do not complain, do not make trouble.

In prayer, I mostly ask God to help me hold this role, not always to free me from it.

Another layer settles into the body here: living in a Black body, under global exposure to racial violence, while carrying the constant pressure to be exemplary. There is no place for all of that tension to rest. It accumulates.

SECTION XI — TOGETHER AGAIN

By late 2020, the distance finally ended. But being in the same place did not mean I had learned a different way to live.

In November 2020, just before Thanksgiving, Kristianna's green card was approved. The long distance chapter finally ended. After years of waiting, applications, interviews, denials, delays, prayers, she was allowed to come home. Not for a visit. Not with uncertainty. Not with a clock ticking above us. But to live with me. Permanently.

I was about to be reunited with the love of my life. It did not feel real or possible. I was excited, relieved, grateful. The long distance was finally ending. And I was anxious, not because I doubted us, but because time apart had shaped us in ways we had never fully named. Our love had deepened but so had the parts of us that had learned to live alone. I wondered what it would mean to merge those versions of ourselves again. I wanted the moment to feel natural, but I knew there was a chance it might feel unfamiliar. I wanted it to be perfect.

The night before, I made a sign. A big one. I wrote, "This is the moment we've been waiting for. I've missed you so much. I love you. Welcome home." I drew a heart, and a basketball in the corner, for reasons I still cannot fully explain. I bought flowers too. I wanted her to feel celebrated, welcomed, held, not as a visitor passing through my life, but as the woman I hoped to build a home with. We still have that sign.

When she walked through the arrivals gate, I rushed into her arms. The embrace was emotional in a way I had not prepared for. Months of distance, longing, paperwork, and screens collapsed into one moment of closeness. I gave her the flowers and the sign. She smiled, not a full, unguarded smile, but a tentative one, and something inside me stirred rather than settled. It was not disappointment. It was the weight of what was now beginning: our life together, in one place, with no departure date. I sensed her own mixture of joy and uncertainty. I asked a stranger to take a picture of us. I did not want the moment to slip through my fingers.

We took an Uber to Ashburnham. The ride felt like sacred ground. We kept the conversation light, how her flight was, how cold it felt outside, what we might eat later, the kind of small talk people reach for when they are stitching their worlds back together. Beneath those simple words, my heart was saying: She's here. She's here. We're not saying goodbye this time.

It was an ordinary day.

And one of the most meaningful days of my life.

But what neither of us fully understood then was how much the years of distance had stretched us. Distance does not simply separate bodies. It rewires the ways we cope, connect, and protect ourselves. Reuniting did not erase that wiring. It simply placed us in the same space again, asking us to relearn rhythms we had once taken for granted. She brought her tenderness. I brought my fatigue. We loved each other deeply, but we were entering a new season, one in which presence would reveal just how much my pace, my pressures, and my inner conflicts had been shaping our relationship.

And even with her by my side, my rhythm did not change.

My responsibilities continued.

My overextension continued.

And my body, already speaking in quiet warnings, kept absorbing what I refused to name.

For the first time in years, geography stopped being the enemy. We shared the same roof. Woke up in the same place. No longer measured our relationship in flights, visas, or departure dates. From the outside, it looked like stability had arrived.

But inside, my rhythm stayed the same. I carried into this new season the habits that had sustained me through instability: speed, vigilance, overfunctioning, emotional restraint. The same calendar logic. The same inability to pause without guilt.

With Kristianna now physically present, what distance had previously masked became visible. She saw the fatigue I minimized. The nights that did not restore me. The way I stayed busy even when nothing urgent demanded it. The way my mind kept running when my body was clearly asking for rest. We had the same address, but not yet the same pace. I was relieved that we were finally together. I was grateful beyond words. But I was also quietly exhausted by the effort of continuing to be strong now that someone could see the cracks.

The conflict deepened: intimacy asks for presence, and I had trained myself to survive without it.

SECTION XII — ASHEVILLE, SAME SCRIPT

The move to Asheville looked like a new chapter. In many ways it was. But inwardly, I kept repeating the same script in a new setting.

In June 2021, I accepted a position at Asheville School in North Carolina, teaching humanities and history. In July 2022, I was appointed Director of Community Engagement, Diversity, and Belonging.

We moved again. New state. New campus. New community.

On paper, everything made sense.

In my spirit, everything grew heavier.

This role resonated deeply with my own story, belonging sought across borders, languages, cultures, and institutions. I believed in the work. I cared about the students. I carried the mission seriously.

But the role was expansive.

Courses in the morning.

Student support throughout the day.

Conflict mediation.

Sensitive conversations.

Faculty meetings.

Community programming.

Evening events.

Coaching.

Emails that arrived faster than they could be answered.

And above all of it, a dissertation that still needed to be finished.

I became increasingly effective, and increasingly absent from myself.

Competent. Reliable. Trusted.

And deeply tired.

Kristianna saw it before I admitted it.

"You're here," she told me gently, "but you're not really here."

She warned me softly at first, then more directly:

"This pace isn't sustainable. One day, either your body or our marriage will pay for it."

I heard her.

I respected her.

I loved her.

But I did not know how to slow down without fear, fear of losing momentum, fear of disappointing others, fear of becoming dispensable, fear that everything I had built depended on my constant motion.

What I could not yet see clearly was this:

God was not pushing me forward here.

He was positioning me near a boundary.

Not to punish me, but to save something more valuable than my résumé.

CONCLUSION — THE BOUNDARY I DID NOT YET SEE

By the time we arrived in Asheville, the rhythm of my life had become something I no longer questioned. It felt normal to carry more than one person should carry. It felt natural to move faster than my body could sustain. It felt responsible to keep going even when fatigue was quietly asking for attention.

From the outside, the structure looked solid.

I had a doctorate in progress.

A meaningful role in a school community.

A marriage that had survived years of distance.

A life that many people would call successful.

From the inside, however, something had already begun to shift.

The rhythm that once felt like faithfulness had slowly become compulsion. The discipline that once helped me endure had hardened into a refusal to pause. And the body that had carried me faithfully across continents, responsibilities, and seasons of ambition had begun sending signals I did not yet understand how to hear.

At the time, I still believed the story was about perseverance.

I did not yet know it was about limits.

I believed strength meant continuing.

I believed faith meant enduring.

I believed that as long as I had not collapsed, everything was still under control.

What I could not yet see was that my body had already entered the conversation.

Quietly at first.

Patiently.

Almost respectfully.

The body negotiates before it rebels.

For years, mine had been negotiating.

I did not yet know that the next stage of this story would no longer be written primarily through choices, responsibilities, or achievements.

It would be written through signals.

Signals that could no longer be postponed, minimized, or explained away.

That is where the next chapter begins.

The rhythm of life had already fractured.

Now the body would begin to speak.

2

WHEN THE BODY BECOMES A MESSENGER

There are seasons when the body tells the truth more cleanly than the mouth.

Before the stroke, I knew how to talk about conflict. I analyzed it. I taught it. I mediated it in other people's lives. I could see it inside organizations, families, and systems. I could name power dynamics, hidden loyalties, and the quiet damage of what is never said. But I did not recognize it when it was happening inside me.

For years, I stayed upright out of habit, out of duty, out of pride. I told myself that as long as I could function, everything was fine. I treated exhaustion as the price of success, of honoring my parents' sacrifices, of holding multiple roles, multiple languages, multiple worlds without dropping any of them.

My body was taking notes in silence.

This chapter is the moment it stopped being polite.

Not with a speech.

Not with a dramatic announcement.

But with signs that, at first, could almost pass as ordinary: fatigue that felt familiar, a signature that refused to form, a hand that no longer recognized its own pen, words that began to stumble on the tongue. These details, stacked inside an ordinary morning in Yaoundé, became a message. Something in me had reached the edge.

Before the stroke became an event, it was already becoming a language.

In Chapter 1, life breaks the rhythm.

Here, the body takes the floor.

SECTION I — THE BODY SPEAKS FIRST

By then, the signs were no longer small. The body had been negotiating for years, and I kept answering with postponement.

Long before it collapses, the body negotiates.

Mine had been negotiating for years.

Since 2014, I had been diagnosed with hypertension. Medication was prescribed. I took it sometimes. Then I stopped. Then I resumed. Then I stopped again. I never made it nonnegotiable. I treated it as something temporary, adjustable, and secondary.

In 2016, shortly after arriving in Florida, blood work revealed elevated glucose levels. The doctors told me to monitor it. I heard the words. I nodded. I did not change the rhythm.

That same year, a sleep study confirmed obstructive sleep apnea. I was given a CPAP machine. At first, I used it diligently. Then inconsistently. Then rarely. Then not at all.

Each diagnosis arrived politely.

Each recommendation was reasonable.

Each intervention assumed I would cooperate.

But cooperation would have required a deeper change, one I was not prepared to make.

By 2023, the word diabetes finally appeared clearly in my chart.

Still, even then, I did not feel sick in the way we imagine illness.

I was functioning.

What I experienced instead were accumulations.

Shortness of breath during short walks.

Dizziness that came and went.

A heart that sometimes beat too loudly, too fast.

Morning exhaustion that sleep did not resolve.

Irritability.

Difficulty concentrating.

Numbness in my hands and feet.

None of these felt dramatic enough to stop.

I learned to manage them.

Even in the classroom, my body adapted in quiet, revealing ways.

I stopped sitting down.

I stayed on my feet the entire period, walking between desks, writing on the board, asking questions. To students, it probably looked like energy, engagement, movement.

In truth, it was fear.

If I sat, I might fall asleep.

If I fell asleep, I would lose control.

If I lost control, the image would crack.

So I stayed upright.

My body was no longer an ally.

It had become something to monitor, to restrain, to silence.

I told myself:

"It's just fatigue."

"This is normal."

"I don't have a choice."

This was not resilience.

It was denial dressed up as discipline.

Kristianna continued to say the same thing, in different words:

"Slow down."

"Listen to your body."

"This isn't healthy."

I heard her.

I loved her.

I kept going anyway.

I believed that because I had not yet collapsed, I must be different. Stronger. Built for this.

I did not realize I was approaching a threshold.

The body does not rebel suddenly. It escalates. It waits. It signals. And when signals are repeatedly ignored, it eventually chooses a language that cannot be negotiated away.

SECTION II — FAITH IN SURVIVAL MODE

Even here, faith remained. But it had changed. It was no longer guiding the pace. It was helping me endure it.

Throughout all of this, my faith never disappeared.

It changed posture.

When I left Cameroon, I believed God had a plan for my life. At first, I thought that plan ran through the NBA. People who know me today, especially those who met me after the stroke, after the doctorate, after the years of work in schools, sometimes have trouble imagining the athlete I once was.

But I was not a typical college kid with a casual affection for the game.

My body was built for basketball, and for a time I lived as though the court itself were the place where God intended to reveal my future.

Even though I am only 6'3" or 6'4", I was listed at 6'5" in high school. I played much bigger than my frame. In Cameroon, that physicality made me stand out early. In the United States, it made me competitive.

By my junior and senior years at New Hampton School, I was between 215 and 220 pounds. In college at UNH, I played at around 240, strong, explosive, able to battle players with national reputations and NBA projections.

I led my high school team in rebounding my junior and senior years and in scoring my junior year.

I was raw in places but gifted. And the body God had given me felt like a promise I was meant to fulfill.

High level programs showed real interest. UConn, Michigan State, Stanford, Miami and others.

For a boy who grew up in Essos, walking onto American soil under the prayers of his family, those moments felt like divine confirmation.

But the body has its own story.

And mine began speaking earlier than I understood.

After my junior year of high school, I suffered the first major injury of my career. The pain in my knee was sharp, persistent, more than the normal wear and tear of the game. They suspected it was my meniscus.

Looking back, I still feel uneasy about what happened next. I was taken to surgery without a proper MRI, an attempt to cut costs, though no one said it out loud. I did not yet have the authority or the language to question the process. I trusted the adults around me. I trusted the system designed to shape athletes.

During the arthroscopic procedure, they found a massive bone spur, far more complicated than expected. It needed careful treatment. It needed structured rehabilitation.

But after the operation, I saw the doctor only once or twice.

There was no real follow up, no physical therapy plan, no specialist guiding my recovery. I had to do my own rehabilitation, relying mostly on a man who lifted weights at New Hampton. He cared about me, but he was not trained for the kind of healing I needed.

The pressure to return was enormous.

I felt responsible to my family, my coaches, my teammates and to the dream that had carried me across an ocean.

So I rushed back.

Too soon.

Underprepared.

Not healed.

And just like that, everything changed.

The offers, the interest, the doors that had once seemed open evaporated almost overnight.

UNH saw an opportunity to sign me, and I loved my official visit there. I made it my home.

But I knew I had stepped onto a different path.

It was a good path, but not the one I had believed would take me to the highest level.

This injury was the first fracture in a dream I had built my identity around.

Over time, the doctorate became the new storyline I attached meaning to.

But during the PhD years, my prayers changed.

They became shorter.

More urgent.

Less relational.

"Lord, give me strength."

"Help me hold on."

"Keep me standing."

What I rarely prayed was:

"Lord, show me what needs to change."

I was not asking God to interrupt my pace.

I was asking Him to sustain it.

My faith shifted into survival mode.

God was not distant.

I was.

SECTION III — DOCTOR ON UNSTEADY LEGS

By 2023, the achievement I had worked toward finally arrived. But it did not arrive in a whole body.

In March 2023, I defended my dissertation.

I became Doctor Onguetou.

On June 9, 2023, I walked across the stage at Nova Southeastern University. My name was read. Hands were shaken. Photographs were taken. Smiles were exchanged. The moment was real, earned, heavy with meaning.

I think of my parents.

Of my mother's constancy in prayer.

Of my father's quiet sacrifices.

Of Yaoundé.

Of the small house in Essos.

Of the years when my success existed only as a hope whispered into faith.

I am proud.

I am grateful.

But I am also exhausted in a way that no ceremony can mask.

If someone had taken me aside that day and asked, without performance or expectation,

"How are you, really?"

The honest answer would have frightened me.

I am tired down to the core.

This fatigue does not resolve with sleep.

It does not respond to weekends.

It lives beneath the surface, structural, constant.

I feel stretched emotionally, physically, spiritually.

Pulled in every direction.

Afraid not of some distant failure, but of collapse in the present.

And still, I say nothing.

I tell myself what I have told myself for years:

"God has carried me this far. He will carry me a little further."

What I did not yet understand was this.

Sometimes God carries us by stopping us.

By then everything was already in place.

Chronic overextension.

Unresolved inner tension.

Relational strain carried silently.

A theology that sustained motion but resisted interruption.

A body whose warnings had become routine noise.

From the outside, this looked like triumph.

From the inside, it felt like a structure held together by momentum alone.

SECTION IV — BEFORE THE BREAK

Then came Cameroon. Home, family, celebration, joy. And beneath the joy, something was already giving way.

On June 24, 2023, Kristianna and I traveled to Cameroon.

A month of celebration lay ahead.

I would present my wife to my family.

We would celebrate the doctorate.

We would rest.

We would reconnect with those who had carried me in prayer for years.

We stayed in an apartment above his house that my brother Jeannot had rented for us.

We spent time with him and his wife Maureen.

With my sister Esther, her husband Hervé and their children.

Most mornings we had breakfast at Jeannot's house. In the afternoon we ate at Esther's.

We traveled to Douala to see my sister Paule, her husband Patrick and their family.

The intention was clear. Joy, presence, restoration.

But my habits did not know how to rest.

I organized a basketball clinic.

I filled the calendar.

I kept moving as if empty space were dangerous.

Rest still felt like betrayal.

Kristianna organized the timing carefully so we could be in Yaoundé on July 11, my mother's birthday. Two days later we were scheduled to leave for Egypt.

On July 11 I led the basketball clinic.

That evening we celebrated my mother.

The house was full.

Laughter rose.

Food circulated.

Photographs were taken.

I smiled.

I spoke.

I remained upright.

But inside something shifted.

This fatigue was different.

Not familiar.

Not manageable.

Not something I could explain away.

It was heavy.

Dense.

Ominous.

I told myself it was just a long day.

That rest would come later.

That tonight belonged to my mother.

We went upstairs to the apartment Jeannot had built above his house. I lay down and thought:

"Tomorrow will be better."

I did not know yet that tomorrow would divide my life in two.

What happened next did not arrive with warning sirens or dramatic collapse. It arrived quietly through a voice that sounded strange, a hand that refused to obey, a signature that would not form.

SECTION V — THE MORNING WITHOUT WARNING

When I replay the hours before the stroke, I do not see big scenes.

I see details.

I remember that morning in Mimboman, in the apartment above Jeannot's place. The day was not fully awake yet, but a gray light was already pushing through the curtains. In the distance you could hear the first horns, motorcycles coughing into motion, the rising voices of pedestrians. Yaoundé coming back to itself.

I got up early.

I had not eaten yet.

My body felt heavy, but nothing about it felt like an emergency. Heaviness had become familiar.

You do not finish a doctorate, live inside overlapping responsibilities and carry multiple communities without accumulating fatigue. That was the story I told myself.

Yves, my mother's driver, arrived to pick us up.

You heard the car before you saw it.

The engine announcing itself.

Then the short horn that says: I am here.

We went downstairs.

The morning air had that fragile coolness that never lasts long in Yaoundé.

I sat in front.

My mother sat in the back.

We left Mimboman for Essos, then toward Elig Essono where the Touristique Express agency was located. We needed to pick up a package my younger sister Paule had sent in my name.

My mother talked.

Advice. Reminders. Blessings. Warnings.

Her voice filled the car with that mix of tenderness and firmness I have known since childhood.

She reminded me, not for the first time, to watch my health.

To stop treating myself like two people inside one body.

Outside, Yaoundé moved in its familiar chaos.

Cars cutting in.

Horns answering horns.

Motorcycles threading themselves through gaps that do not exist.

Inside, I felt tired.

The way I always felt.

Nothing that seemed entirely new.

That morning, I had no reason to believe my life was about to split.

No dramatic warning.

No sharp pain.

Just a thin veil over my attention that I had learned to normalize.

If I had known my body was already writing a message I would not be able to ignore, I might have listened differently.

But that day, to me, it was simply another morning in a life that moved too fast.

SECTION VI — THE SIGNATURE

We arrived at the Touristique Express agency in Elig Essono.

The choreography of buses, parcels and passengers was already underway.

Someone handed me a paper.

"Sign here."

A normal gesture.

I took the pen.

I leaned forward.

I started to write.

And something slipped.

The letters would not follow.

My hand stopped in the middle of the movement.

My line tilted off course.

My first thought was simple.

What is happening? Try again.

I tried again.

But the pen felt foreign, as if I had never held one before.

Radar Onguetou.

My own name.

Refused to be written.

I told my mother I could not write.

She understood I was not joking.

She signed for me, I believe.

And then I said something that came from deep inside my upbringing.

“Mama, I think I am being attacked.”

My mother placed her hand on me and began to pray.

God is in control.

If God is for you who can be against you?

No weapon formed against you will prosper.

As she prayed, a cold shiver crossed my body.

Sharp.

Sudden.

Unmistakable.

My hand, unable to write my own name, had become the first messenger of the fracture forming inside me.

SECTION VII — DISCONNECTION

Most days, I cannot even tell you exactly where stress lives in my body. Maybe in my back when it tightens. Maybe in my sleep when I wake up still exhausted.

Since September 2016, I had officially known I had sleep apnea. I knew my heart raced when my head was full. Reports, machines, numbers, medicine had already given names to some things.

But this was not that.

This was disconnection.

My brain said: write.

My hand refused.

My brain said: move.

My legs hesitated.

This was no longer a gentle warning. Not "you're stressed; pay attention."

This was an emergency signal. A break between intention and execution.

As if the internal command chain had snapped and the orders were failing to reach the limbs.

I had never lived that before.

And that is what frightened me.

And still, in the same old reflex, I minimized.

It's weird... but it will pass.

That minimization, I now recognize, was part of the pattern: the body shouts, and we answer as if it is only whispering.

SECTION VIII — MY MOTHER'S PRAYER

After praying, my mother looked at me with that mixture of gentleness and gravity I know well. She did not interrogate me. She did not dramatize. She held me in that space between human fear and trust in God.

She suggested we go see an herbalist in Omnisports, a neighborhood in Yaoundé.

In our context, that reflex is old. When something is wrong, you go where people have gone before. You try what is familiar. You try what has helped others.

We went.

The car swallowed the distance from Elig Essono to Omnisports through Yaoundé's undisciplined traffic. Outside, the city continued: vendors, students in uniform, taxis stopping anywhere.

When the therapist received us, I was still in shock. I did not understand what was happening, but I knew it was not a simple discomfort.

I tried to explain my symptoms: the inability to write, the strange sensation in my head, the fatigue that felt different.

I did not complain about my stomach. I said nothing about digestion.

He gave me remedies for digestion anyway.

We went back to the apartment above Jeannot's house.

That apartment, days earlier, had symbolized lightness, vacation, a temporary nest. It began to change function. It became an in-between place: between the body before and the body after.

I told Kristianna everything, the signature, the shiver, the visit.

She listened. She watched my face. She saw something that did not look like ordinary fatigue.

Without saying it outright, she had already begun to fear that something close to a stroke, or at least something living near that threshold, was unfolding in my body. She did not have the medical word for it, but she felt the gravity. She has always been intuitive with my body, often noticing shifts in me before I can name them myself. While I tried to minimize what was happening, she was already holding a truth I could not yet accept, and I know she was hoping, strongly, desperately, that she was wrong.

She told me to rest and said she would begin preparing our bags for the Egypt trip scheduled two days later.

I lay down.

I tried again to write my name.

There was a small improvement, just enough to fool me.

But it still was not normal. The letters slid away from my will.

The night that followed was hard.

I slept poorly.

I woke up more exhausted than the day before.

Later Kristianna told me something that still stings when I remember it:

"You were there, but you weren't you. Your eyes were empty. You looked at me without seeing me, like I didn't exist."

That morning, she understood before I did that this was not normal. She tried to stay calm, but inside, a deep fear rose.

She pushed for us to go to a clinic.

Something was already playing out between our perceptions: me, still minimizing; her, sensing that the border of it'll be fine had already been crossed.

SECTION IX — THE ROAD TO NKOMKANA

On the drive to the clinic in Nkomkana, what I remember most is silence.

Not peaceful silence.

Weighted silence.

I remember the road. The piles of trash by the side. The sounds of the city that continued as if nothing had shifted: calls of vendors, motorcycles, animated conversations at the edge of the street.

The outside world did not know what was happening inside my head and body.

A city does not slow down for one man, even when his life is splitting.

I do not remember exactly what my mother was doing, but I would not be surprised if she was murmuring prayers under her breath.

I do not recall every detail of Kristianna's face, but I remember her controlled calm.

I can imagine what this meant for her: being in a country she did not fully know, in a health system whose language and codes were not hers, carrying the fear of losing me, and the fear of not knowing how to save me.

No one in the car said the word stroke.

No one said, "This is serious."

But inside that silence, each of us was trying to understand what was happening.

I felt strangely undone.

Not just tired.

Undone, as if I had lost a battle I did not even know I was fighting.

Undone, as if I no longer wanted to fight, only to lay down my weapons and rest without thinking about tomorrow.

This was no longer Radar, the organizer, the planner, the one who holds everything.

This was a man being driven, literally and spiritually, because he no longer had the strength to steer.

That heavy silence between Mokolo and Nkomkana was already the body taking control. It was the first crack in my illusion of mastery.

SECTION X — THE DOCTOR AND THE IV

At the Nkomkana clinic, the doctor received me.

His face was calm, serious, focused, careful. Not panicked. Not indifferent.

He asked questions.

I wanted to answer.

But when I tried to speak, my voice betrayed me.

Words stumbled.

I slurred.

Simple sentences required enormous effort.

I could hear my own voice sounding blurred, as if someone had placed a filter over my speech.

Kristianna sat beside me. She listened to what I said and what I could not say. She translated, filled gaps, carried the conversation like a bridge between my clear mind and my unraveling speech.

I felt a weakness I did not recognize.

My head spun.

It looked as if things were moving when they were not.

This is where I felt, deeply, that I was no longer in control.

It was not a precise moment I can timestamp. It was a sensation: a fall you cannot reverse by simply tightening your jaw.

I often told my players:

"When you fall, you get back up. There's no time to feel sorry for yourself."

Here I had fallen, and I did not have the means to rise.

They took my blood pressure.

It was through the roof.

They put me on an IV. They gave me medication to bring it down. A nurse checked my vitals repeatedly, nearly every hour.

Later, Kristianna told me they thought they were preventing a stroke, while the stroke had already happened.

In certain papers, people would mention a transient ischemic attack. Doctors in the U.S. would later confirm it was a stroke.

In the moment, I did not think about those terms.

I thought only this:

I want someone to take care of me.

I can't do this anymore.

Something shifted in my inner posture. I was no longer the one who carried everything. I became the one being carried. For my ego, that was violence. But strangely, it was also relief.

It was a hinge between the man who forced himself upright for years and the man who, without giving himself permission, finally stopped.

When the nurse checked my vitals again, tightening the IV line, I realized I had crossed into a place I could no longer manage. Whatever was happening inside my body had already outrun my ability to control it. I was being carried into the moment, not steering it.

INTERLUDE — A QUIET FEAR

I was afraid to die, even if I refused to say the words. The thought stayed at the edges of my mind like a shadow I would not turn toward. But the fear of death was not the sharpest feeling. The shock of what my body was doing was heavier, louder, more disorienting. The shock of realizing that I was not invincible, and that my life could tilt without warning in a country where water barely ran and mosquitoes circled the ceiling, felt more immediate than the fear of dying itself.

I tried not to imagine the worst: Is this where it ends? Is this how my story closes?

But the possibility hovered. It stayed close, but not strong enough to take over. What took over was exhaustion, deep, relentless, numbing. I was so tired that it muted every other emotion, even fear. The body was fighting one battle; my mind was fighting another.

This kind of fear is hard to describe. It was not panic. It was not denial. It was standing at a threshold I had not chosen, aware that one wrong step could shift everything, and yet too depleted to argue with the moment. I did not want to die. But I did not have the strength to resist the thought. Fatigue, not fear, was the clearest message that day.

SECTION XI — THE CT SCAN

By the time Kristianna convinced the doctor to order a CT scan, I had stopped trying to hold myself together. Whatever the truth was, it was already unfolding inside me. All I could do now was follow where my body was leading.

The next day, we returned to Omnisports, this time not for plants or remedies, but for images of my brain. Jeannot helped me into the car. Later, Kristianna explained that we traveled in two vehicles. In the first, my sister Esther drove, with Maureen in the front passenger seat and Kristianna in the back beside me. In the second, Jeannot and my mother followed closely behind.

I could barely walk when we arrived. Moving through the hallway felt unreal, as if my feet touched the ground without belonging to it. My balance had become fragile. I felt suspended, untethered, drifting inside a body that no longer held its own weight. Kristianna supported me on one side. I know someone else held me on the other, but that face has faded in my memory. Only the outline remains, like a shadow of care.

They guided me into the imaging area, and I sat in the waiting room among other patients and their families. Each person carried a different worry, yet the expression was the same, the look of people suspended between what they fear and what they hope, waiting for a verdict that could alter their lives.

As I waited, a quiet defeat settled over me. It was not dramatic. It was the slow collapse of something inside, a realization that I could no longer pretend to stand on my own strength. I knew why we were there, but everything around that purpose felt strange, distorted, as if the world had shifted slightly and left me behind. Waves of dizziness rose and fell. My tongue felt unbearably heavy, foreign in my own mouth. When I tried to speak, the words tumbled out unevenly, like someone striking piano keys without knowing the notes. Embarrassment was there, but it was not the dominant feeling. What stayed with me was the sense of being absent from myself. A ghost walking. A man observing his own life from a small distance.

What wounded me most in that moment was not fear. It was the sense of being undone. I had guided students, players, colleagues, and even family members through their storms. Now I needed to be guided simply to take a few steps. The reversal unsettled something deep in me. Sitting in that room, I sensed that the body was no longer whispering. It was delivering its message with unmistakable clarity.

I watched the people around me, each waiting for their own news, each holding a private story of pain, uncertainty, or hope. The sameness in their eyes felt like a mirror. I was no longer the strong one passing through. I was part of that community of the vulnerable, stripped of certainty and held only by the prayers and presence of those beside me.

In that waiting room, I felt, for the first time in years, what it meant to be fully fragile. Exhausted. Transparent. And yet, even in that state, I sensed something quiet holding me together. Not a polished thought or a rehearsed theology, just a steady inner reminder that even when flesh and will give way, there is a strength that remains. It came to me the way breath returns after a long pause, simple, grounding, enough to keep me from unraveling.

When the technician finally called my name, he tried to speak to me, perhaps to offer comfort or instruction. I do not remember what he said. It was as if my mind had detached, surrendering the constant effort to stay composed. I did not have strength for long prayers, just one simple plea: Lord, have mercy on me.

They placed me into the machine. I lay still, staring at the ceiling while the ring circled my head. I thought of my wife, my parents, my family, and the future that suddenly felt fragile. When the scan ended, we returned to the clinic.

The result confirmed what my body had already declared: I had suffered a stroke.

I was hospitalized. In my memory, the stay felt like thirteen days, but in truth it was eight, eight days that were enough to shift the ground beneath me. The confirmation did not bring panic. It arrived like weight. Truth laid bare. A stripping.

What had lived for years as tension between fatigue and will, prayer and worry, image and reality, now appeared in a medical report. The body had spoken in its own language, clear, unambiguous, undeniable.

SECTION XII — THE ROOM

I remember the hospital room with a strange clarity.

It was spacious, with two beds. At night, Kristianna slept on the other bed. My mother laid a mat on the floor and slept there, as if she refused the idea that her son could be hospitalized without her being in the room.

My father came in the afternoons and stayed until late.

Esther, Jeannot, Hervé, Maureen came regularly, morning or daytime.

Esther and Hervé's children, Nathan, Céleste, Kino, Loïs, took turns visiting.

The room was large enough to hold five or six people at once during the day.

There was a small, attached bathroom, but water cuts were common. We used buckets: one to flush, one to wash.

There was no fan.

Mosquitoes hovered.

It was not hell, but it was not comfort.

The bed was small. My muscles pulled, as if my body wanted to escape itself, and yet I had no energy to move. Every movement was calculated. I asked myself whether turning to my side was worth the cost.

Around me, a small community formed: my wife, my family, a few caregivers. Each played their role. Some talked. Some prayed. Some stayed silent.

I discovered what it means to become the involuntary center of attention.

I, who always kept others at the center of my concern, students, players, colleagues, family, became the case around which everyone organized.

There was tension even inside those walls: between gratitude for being surrounded and discomfort at taking up space; between my desire to stay discreet and the reality of dependence.

SECTION XIII — LAYING DOWN THE WEAPONS

The first night, I was not afraid the way people imagine.

No cinematic flashback.

No life replaying itself.

I was mostly relieved to be there, relieved that no one had dismissed it as nothing.

I do not even remember how every decision was made. I only remember that after the scan I was back on an IV with other treatments.

I felt like a soldier finally laying down his weapons, accepting that today's battle was over, that I could not remain standing.

I did not spend the night negotiating with God.

I did not inventory my regrets.

I mostly rested.

Despite the nurse's visits, the blood pressure checks, injections, the trips to the bathroom with help, my sleep was light, but it was gentle.

I did not feel good.

But I was not fighting my body anymore.

For the first time in a long time, I was not forcing myself to keep going at all costs.

That night, I touched a truth I would need years to fully articulate:

Sometimes the first act of healing is simply laying down the weapons.

SECTION XIV — HUMILIATION AND DIGNITY

Among the moments of those eight days, one struck my ego with force:

The bathing.

From the second day onward, and through the rest of my stay, Kristianna washed me.

It was the first and only time in my adult life that another adult, and especially my wife, washed me like you wash a baby.

I felt shame.

A quiet shame, steady, stubborn.

It returned each time, even though I knew it was irrational.

I felt as if I had failed to be the man I thought I had to be: autonomous, capable, strong.

And yet, in the same movement, something essential happened.

I began to understand that my dignity did not depend on what my body could do, how many miles I could run, how many games I could coach, how many hours I could grind.

My dignity lived somewhere else:

In whom I was when everything I knew how to do collapsed.

After the bath, Kristianna always tried to get me to eat. I could barely swallow anything beyond fruit and soup. Everything else felt too heavy, as if my body no longer had energy to digest.

That tension, between humiliation and dignity, dependence and love received, was part of what the illness exposed.

My body was forcing me to face a question I had avoided for years:

Who are you when you can no longer impress anyone?

Who are you when you need to be carried, washed, fed?

I did not yet have the words.

But the question had been planted.

SECTION XV — SILENCE, SPEECH, AND SONG

During those hospital days, I did not try to speak much.

Not because I did not want to, but because every word demanded too much.

I feared opening my mouth and hearing blurred sounds, broken syllables, language I did not recognize coming out of me.

So I chose silence.

Not because I imagined a future without speech.

I refused to go that far in my mind.

I watched Kristianna's eyes and saw how hard she worked to understand me even when I spoke little. The way she stayed with me inside the blur gave me deep comfort. I did not feel like a prisoner trapped in my body, pounding on glass, unheard.

I felt exhausted, but not entirely absent.

I slept a lot.

I woke up, watched, slept again.

One day my mother invited men from their church to pray for me.

They entered, set down their things, and began to sing hymns in French.

I knew these songs. They belonged to my spiritual memory.

And there, while speech was difficult, I realized I could sing.

The words came out clearly. Cleanly.

I sang almost perfectly.

Kristianna was shaken. She said with something close to joy:

"You're singing. You're singing normally. I can hear you."

That small victory gave me an amount of hope disproportionate to its size.

I did not know whether I would regain my speech the way it used to be.

But I knew something in me could still express itself.

I was not entirely foreign to my own voice.

And deeper still, without fully formulating it, I saw another layer of what was happening:

Where functional speech stumbled, singing, speech aimed toward God, still passed through.

As if, in the chaos, worship remained an intact corridor.

SECTION XVI — WHEN THE BODY REVEALS WHAT HAS BEEN HIDDEN

Looking back, I see clearly: the stroke did not create what was broken in me. It revealed it.

It exposed it like harsh light entering a room I had kept deliberately dim.

The first fracture was between my rhythm and my real needs.

I lived as if my energy were infinite, as if my body were a tool placed in service of ambition and responsibility.

For years I told myself:

“I don’t have a choice.”

My body had been answering quietly with the opposite truth.

Until the day it stopped whispering and began to shout.

The second fracture lived between my declared faith and my hidden fear.

I proclaimed God’s faithfulness, yet part of me believed I had to remain strong to be worthy of the opportunities placed before me.

Without realizing it, I had turned faith into endurance.

The stroke cracked that theology.

The third fracture lived between image and reality.

The image: the disciplined man, the coach, the director, the reliable husband.

The reality: a tired man unable to say, “I have reached my limit.”

The stroke removed the stage set.

It left the stage bare.

When inner tensions have no language, they eventually search for another one.

Often, the body becomes that language.

My stroke was not only a biological rupture.

It was also a message.

A red light.

A language I could no longer avoid.

And yet the stroke did not immediately create a new life.

It only ended the illusion that the old one could continue unchanged.

Something in me had begun to die.

The version of myself who believed everything rested on my strength.

The version who did not know how to ask for help.

The version who survived instead of inhabiting his life.

If I wanted to live, really live, I could not continue as before.

The deeper work had only begun.

CONCLUSION — LEAVING THE CLINIC

I left the Nkomkana clinic on July 22.

The sun was high. The city continued its life, indifferent to what I had just lived.

I walked more slowly, but I walked.

I spoke more slowly, but I spoke.

And yet everything in me had changed.

The body I inhabited that day was no longer the body I thought I knew.

It looked like mine. It had my skin, my hands, my gait.

But it did not obey in the same way.

It sent different signals.

It demanded a different respect.

We returned to Jeannot's apartment, no longer a vacation place, but a waiting room between the man before and the man after.

This chapter ends where the longer work begins.

In the return.

In the in-between.

In the moment you understand that surviving is not yet healing.

Because when the body speaks, the heart must answer.

And sometimes, that is where the real storm begins.

3

THE INNER STORM

The Return to an Unfamiliar Body

There is a moment after a crisis when the body finally stops fighting, but the soul is only beginning to understand what happened.

In Yaoundé, my body spoke louder than everything else. It protested. It gave out. It sent signals I could no longer afford to ignore. When I say the body became the messenger, I am not reaching for poetry. I am naming what happened. An overloaded body made a decision I refused to make.

But once the noise of the emergency settled, something else appeared. Less visible. Less spectacular than a scan or a diagnosis. More disorienting.

That is where this chapter begins.

This chapter is a bridge between two fractures: the body's fracture, brutal, measurable, medical; and the inner fracture, quieter, more diffuse, but just as real. The inner storm.

If Chapter 1 tells how the rhythm of my life began to crack, and Chapter 2 tells how my body became the stage where that conflict could no longer hide, Chapter 3 tells what happened when I returned home and discovered that home did not feel the same, because I did not feel the same.

SECTION I — HOME SWEET HOME

Home sweet home.

The words rose out of me on their own, almost like a prayer my body whispered before I understood I had spoken.

I let myself sink into the large couch in our living room. My body felt heavy, emptied out, as if gravity had increased somewhere between Atlanta and Asheville. Everything in me demanded a pause. My muscles. My head. My nerves. My heart.

I was home, but I could not find myself inside my own home.

Looking back, I understand that moment was not only the end of a trip. It was a landing inside a body I no longer recognized. Those three words were not a joke. They were an exhale. The exhale of a man who had passed through a whirlwind that was geographical, medical, familial, and spiritual, and who could finally touch ground without yet knowing whether he could trust that ground.

To understand the weight of that exhale, you have to go back a few days earlier. Back to July 22, 2023. Back to the moment they let me leave the clinic in Cameroon.

On paper, it was good news. I was stable enough to leave. I walked out with a battered body, a traumatized brain, a fractured identity, and a voice that could not keep up with the thoughts inside me.

My mind had not caught up with what my body had endured.

This is where the inner storm begins: in the gap between what can be seen and what is lived, between returning home and the intimate sense of no longer inhabiting the same body.

And this is where what I call conflict–illness theory begins to unfold, not first as a concept, but as a lived reality. Illness is not only a medical episode. It is also a site of conflict. Conflict between body and mind. Conflict between systems of care. Conflict between old identities and new fragilities. Conflict between what others expect from you and what you can give.

But when I collapsed onto that couch and whispered home sweet home, I could not name any of that yet. I knew only one thing.

I am home.

And yet I do not recognize myself.

SECTION II — LEAVING THE CLINIC

They let me leave the clinic on July 22, after eight days in the hospital.

Jeannot came to pick us up. We returned to the apartment above his house in Mimboman. At first, that apartment was supposed to be a temporary base for joy. Celebrating my dissertation. Seeing family. Breathing the country again. Preparing for what came next.

It became something else. A corridor between two worlds. The world before the stroke and the world after.

I was emptied out. More than tired. Like a soldier who has put down his weapon without knowing whether the battle is truly over.

From that moment on, Kristianna took over everything.

She made sure I ate. She helped me sit, stand, and lie down. She monitored my medication. She spoke with my family. She handled conversations. She filtered worries. She softened awkwardness. She became my arms, my legs, my memory, and often my voice.

And I rested.

I had nothing left to offer but that. Letting myself be carried.

The day after my discharge, with her encouragement, I managed to go to the bathroom by myself. A small thing to the outside world. To me, it was a victory.

The next day, I managed to bathe by myself. Again, nothing spectacular on the surface. But in my body, it was a small reconquest.

I did not know it then, but this is where the theory began writing itself in my flesh before it would ever appear on paper.

For years, I had done everything to avoid depending on anyone. I built my value on my ability to help, to carry, to absorb, to give. I was the man who handled things. The man who reassured. The man who took it on.

After the stroke, the first lesson was the opposite.

Learning to be served.

Accepting assistance.

Letting someone else carry what I could no longer carry.

My body forced me to experience a truth my mind had resisted for a long time. Strength is not proven only by what you carry. It is also proven by what you are willing to let others carry for you.

And still, even in dependence, I felt another tension. I wanted control. I wanted to choose when help would be offered, how much, and at what cost to my image. I wanted to recover quickly enough to protect the version of myself I had spent years constructing.

But illness does not negotiate with reputation.

It comes with terms.

Slowness.

Humility.

Surrender.

SECTION III — THE URGENCY TO LEAVE

Very quickly, in Kristianna's mind, one thing became non-negotiable.

We needed to return to the United States as soon as possible.

For her, it was out of the question that I remain in Cameroon for long after a stroke. It was not a judgment against my country or my family. It was a precise conviction. I needed structured medical follow-up. Coherent care. In a system she knew, whose codes she understood, where she could advocate for me without constantly translating, negotiating, or justifying.

Later, she told me my mother had suggested I stay in Cameroon for six months to recover.

Six months.

In my mother's logic, it made sense. Family around. Constant presence. Home care. Remedies. Massages. Visits. A full house. Time that stretches.

For Kristianna, it was unthinkable.

And for me too.

I could say I was torn between two loyalties, my mother and my wife. That would sound like a neat conflict narrative. It would also be false.

The truth is that I had no inner dilemma about this. I knew where my place was.

With my wife. At home.

In a medical system where she knew I would be treated correctly.

There were no competing cultural codes in my head. No immigrant identity torn between two worlds. No sense of being in the middle.

There was a simple, clean, almost brutal conviction: my married life would not remain thousands of miles away while I was kept in another country.

The stroke did not blur my priorities.

It clarified them.

What I did see clearly, though, was the collision between the two women who loved me most in this world.

On one side, my mother, with an African logic of care. Presence. Duration. The collective. The belief that healing comes when everyone is there.

On the other side, Kristianna, with a structured logic of care. Appointments. Records. Protocols. Specialists. A coherent pathway.

Two ways of loving.

Two ways of protecting.

Two ways of taking care of one body.

The theorist in me could have pointed and said, here is a conflict between systems of care. But I was too exhausted to mediate anything. I could see the tension, and I could not absorb it the way I used to.

That belongs inside the conflict–illness framework too. There are tensions you can no longer carry. And when you cannot carry them, your body carries the cost.

SECTION IV — A PLACE TO LAND

While those tensions moved through the air, another concrete reality imposed itself.

We could not stay indefinitely in Jeannot's apartment. The reservation was over. The space above his house was never meant to become a long-term recovery room.

My mother insisted we leave that apartment. In her view, the neighborhood was not good. Not safe enough. Not suitable for our situation.

Time pressure. Housing constraints. Medical uncertainty. Family sensitivities. Fatigue.

Everything blended into one another.

In another context, this could have become open conflict. Family. Marriage. Culture. Pride. But I had neither breath nor voice nor inner availability for that.

Again, I felt the pattern.

If I tried to carry all of it, my body would pay the bill.

SECTION V — THE HOTEL

Kristianna found a solution that was both simple and complex.

She organized our return step by step.

She booked flights: Yaoundé to Addis Ababa to Frankfurt with an overnight layover, then Atlanta, then Asheville.

While we waited to leave, she found a hotel in Yaoundé, Hotel ISIS in Odza, not far from Nsimalen Airport. One room for the two of us. Another for my parents. Three nights.

To everyone else, it was a few days at a hotel.

To me, those three days had one purpose:

Regain enough strength for the journey to be possible, without drawing attention to how fragile I really was.

The first afternoon, we went down to the restaurant.

And that is where something unexpected appeared.

The room was almost empty, and yet I felt as if every eye was on me. Ordering a meal, something I had done a thousand times, became an ordeal.

My tongue no longer cooperated. I knew what I wanted to say, but the words jammed. My sentences did not come out the way they existed in my mind. I was also fighting fatigue, a light dizziness, and the strange unsteadiness of a body that could move but could not hold itself for long.

I, who had always been comfortable in public, felt shy.

Not shy like a personality trait. Shy like exposure. Shy like someone whose mask has slipped and who can feel the world noticing.

As if the slightest hesitation in my voice would reveal to everyone that something in me had broken.

I did not tell Kristianna.

I could already see her carrying the hospital, the logistics, my family, our departure, her own emotions, and a culture she was still learning to navigate. I did not want to add one more weight.

And now I am afraid to speak to people.

So I did what I had trained myself to do for years.

I kept inside what hurt the most.

This is one of the quiet violences of illness. It does not only affect the body. It shakes identity.

The confident man becomes hesitant.

The outgoing man becomes guarded.

The voice that used to lead becomes a voice that wants to hide.

My body was sending a message I was not ready to hear.

You will no longer be able to rely on your role.

You will have to face who you are when you cannot perform.

SECTION VI — BEING APART

In those days, my mother arranged for food to be brought in from outside. It was her way of taking back some control over my recovery.

So we went down to the restaurant with our own dishes. We used the hotel plates, the tables, the space, but we did not order anything except water or coffee.

The staff watched us with heavy curiosity.

Nothing openly cruel. But enough insistence in the looks for me to feel that old sensation again.

Being apart.

In normal circumstances, I might have found the scene amusing. In my state, it reinforced the feeling of being out of place, observed, sometimes judged.

Since the stroke, my appetite had shrunk. Fruit and soup became my closest allies.

My mother also arranged massage sessions for me in the room. Her way of caring was tactile. Body. Warmth of hands. A care that says healing is also something you touch.

During those massages, I did nothing. I decided nothing. I carried nothing. I received.

And receiving, for the man I had been, was almost a spiritual exercise.

There was embarrassment.

And gratitude.

Embarrassment to see myself reduced to this state. Gratitude to see how many forms love can take. A vigilant wife. A relentless mother. Family mobilized without hesitation.

Under it all, another tension lived.

Part of me enjoyed being surrounded.

Another part of me resisted, ashamed to need all of it.

SECTION VII — THE TRIP BECOMES A NIGHTMARE

After three nights at the hotel, departure day came.

I could say I was mainly sad to leave my family and my country. That would sound noble.

The truth is simpler.

I wished this trip had never happened.

A month earlier, coming back to Cameroon with my wife, celebrating my doctorate, seeing my parents and siblings, leaving for Egypt, it all felt like a dream.

By departure day, the dream had turned into a nightmare.

A stroke. Nights in a clinic. Injections. Fear. Humiliations. Family tensions. Misunderstandings. Silent tears.

I was disgusted by what I had lived through.

I was not making a vow to never return.

But I wanted this chapter to end.

SECTION VIII — THE SPILLED COFFEE

That morning at the hotel, Kristianna made coffee as she did every morning. She poured me some into a disposable cup.

I spilled it.

Coffee ran onto the floor and the table.

She handed me napkins.

My father, who saw the scene, asked her why she was not doing it herself. In his logic, especially after what had happened to me, it was obvious. She should take care of me down to the smallest detail, including cleaning up what I had spilled.

She answered, controlled but firm, that I would handle it.

In that small incident, something deeper was playing out.

Two visions of marriage.

Two representations of masculinity.

Two conceptions of illness and dignity.

And me in the middle, with spilled coffee and a right hand I no longer recognized.

Even before the stroke, I had always been a little clumsy. Spilling a drink was not extraordinary.

But this time, there was something else.

A heaviness.

A slowness.

A new imprecision.

I could have blamed it on fatigue.

Deep down, I knew it was not only that.

I did not tell Kristianna. I did not want to worry her more.

I filed the fear under later again.

SECTION IX — THE TAXI AND THE CLASH OF WORLDS

To get to the airport, Kristianna called a taxi.

In Yaoundé, traffic can turn a simple crossing into a marathon. She wanted to leave early, build in margin, and avoid unnecessary stress.

My mother disagreed. Feeling unheard, she began to scold Kristianna.

I did not like it.

With the little strength I had, I asked my mother to stop.

I told her calmly that taking the taxi was an excellent idea.

It was not only a practical stance. It was a message.

Trust her.

Right now, she is holding the reins.

Kristianna was furious.

I knew it was not easy for her to face my parents, who can be very direct, very certain in their opinions, convinced their way is best, and sometimes harsh in how they express it.

The art of delicacy is not always what we practice most, especially under stress.

I could see what Kristianna was carrying beyond the stroke itself. Our departure. The bookings. The payments. Navigating a system she did not know. Communicating with my family. And the reality that once back in the U.S., she would reorganize her life around my recovery.

That morning, I saw her love as labor.

Not romantic labor. Real labor. The labor of carrying someone whose body is not cooperating, while staying steady enough for both of you.

SECTION X — NSIMALEN: RELIEF AND GUILT

The taxi arrived, but my mother was not ready despite the agreed time. We decided to leave and let my parents meet us at the airport.

We paid the hotel bill with our credit card. At the time, I did not fully realize how much Kristianna was managing without cash, without easy access to local systems, with limited Wi-Fi, under pressure.

Looking back, the fact that she found tickets, a hotel, payment methods, and a workable itinerary feels like a logistical miracle.

The drive to Nsimalen was calm. The driver respected traffic laws, rare enough at home to deserve mentioning.

At the airport, we checked in. Hervé was there, my sister's husband. Back home, we say someone has weight when they have influence, someone who can intervene if things get complicated.

We did not need it, but his presence soothed something in me.

The moment of goodbye came.

I would like to say I was mainly sad.

The truth is, I had to control my face so my relief would not show.

I wanted to get on that plane. I wanted to leave a country where catastrophe had found me. I wanted to go home.

Inside the airport, the crowd overwhelmed me, not only visually, but physically. I felt oppressed. I wanted to hide. I wanted to disappear into a corner.

I surprised myself thinking, I have become a coward.

I did not tell Kristianna, but I am almost sure she saw that something had shifted in the way I stood among people.

Two hours later, we boarded for Addis Ababa.

As soon as the plane took off, the first clear words that came out of my mouth were simple.

Finally.

Finally out.

And right behind that relief came guilt, because relief can feel like betrayal when it involves your own country.

That mixture belongs to the inner storm.

SECTION XI — ADDIS ABABA: FEAR OF ANOTHER STROKE

The flight to Addis Ababa was difficult.

Since the stroke, I had consumed no sugar. Out of fear. Out of control. Out of the instinct not to make things worse.

On the plane, I refused to eat. I saw sugar, sauces, unfamiliar foods, and I mistrusted all of it.

My blood sugar dropped.

I felt terrible. I struggled to breathe. My legs felt paralyzed. I could barely walk.

I was terrified of having another stroke in a foreign airport, far from any familiar reference.

Kristianna asked for a wheelchair. They took us to the infirmary. Two nurses welcomed us, calm and steady. They checked my vitals and asked questions.

Kristianna avoided saying that I had suffered a stroke two weeks earlier. Instinct, strategy, or simply the sense that saying too much could complicate things.

The nurses recommended one simple thing.

Eat.

We went to a restaurant. I ate a salad and a hamburger. I felt better almost immediately.

And then I saw the truth.

In fear, I had turned my body into an enemy I needed to control at all costs.

By refusing food, I thought I was protecting myself.

I was putting myself in danger.

Health is not war against yourself.

Somewhere between Addis Ababa and Frankfurt, I learned that the hard way.

SECTION XII — FRANKFURT: CONTRAST AND QUIET ENVY

We arrived in Frankfurt late morning. Passport control. Questions. Short answers. A stamp.

We collected our bags and took a taxi to a hotel near the airport.

It had rained. The sky was gray. The air was cool. The streets were clean.

The contrast with what I had just lived for more than a month in Cameroon was brutal.

While there, I caught myself wondering:

Was it like this when I lived here?

Or am I seeing everything differently now?

I thought about the piles of trash, broken roads, water cuts.

I wondered how people adapt to those realities and keep moving as if nothing is happening.

And inside that contrast, another question surfaced.

Am I betraying my own country for feeling relief here?

I had no clean answer. I knew only that, in that moment, it felt good to be in Germany.

At the hotel, I wanted sleep. Only sleep.

Sleep—and more sleep.

Kristianna did not feel well. She chewed raw ginger and garlic and lay down. For her, getting sick was not an option. Too much was resting on her shoulders.

That afternoon, her mother joined us.

We went down to eat together. I could barely speak. Words were rare. So I let them talk in German.

I did not understand the language, but I understood love through looks, gestures, and the quiet familiarity between them.

Her mother turned to me and spoke in English with simple words and gestures. She told me to take my time. That she believed I would heal. That one day this would become a bad memory.

She loves me deeply. I love her too.

When it was time to say goodbye, she kissed me with tenderness that felt almost maternal. Then she wrapped her daughter in her arms.

For a few seconds, I saw Kristianna as a child in her mother's embrace.

And I felt something in me that surprised me.

Envy.

Not jealous envy. Not bitter envy.

A longing.

Watching them brought me back to the relationship I used to have with my own mother before 2004. Back when I told her everything. Fears. Desires. Small victories. Defeats too. No filter.

Then the plane happened. The departure. The silent promise never to worry her. And without noticing, I started calling only when things were going well. I wanted to be her pride, not her anxiety. I shared wins, not struggles. I sterilized the relationship.

Seeing Kristianna with her mother stirred a desire to return to that honesty.

It made me want to return to the honesty I once had with my mother—to become again that son who is not afraid to say:

Mom, today I am not okay.

And it also stirred another desire.

I wanted to become that kind of presence for Kristianna.

She opens her heart without calculation. She tells me what she feels—the beautiful, the hard, the ambiguous, the uncomfortable.

In that hotel restaurant, I understood clearly that I had not always been a safe space for her. Not because I did not love her, but because I did not know how to let emotional truth live in the room without trying to manage it, solve it, or silence it.

And there, quietly, a knot in the conflict–illness framework showed itself.

When you have no place to lay down what weighs on you, the body becomes that place.

When you have no person with whom to be true, the body speaks in your place.

I asked myself questions I did not yet know how to answer.

How do I relearn emotional honesty?

How do I build that with her, and with myself too?

How do I become the man who says what is wrong before the cliff?

I did not know it then, but that question would become essential to the recovery that followed.

SECTION XIII — THE LAST FLIGHT

The night passed quickly. Morning came. Frankfurt to Atlanta to Asheville.

Frankfurt Airport was crowded. Again, the urge to hide. Again, the urge to disappear.

I narrowed my world to Kristianna. Follow her steps. Attach myself to her rhythm in a place saturated with noise.

She checked bags. Secured tickets. Managed the transitions.

The flight from Frankfurt to Atlanta was the best segment. We were not seated together, but she made sure I had a more comfortable seat. She spent money to make the journey survivable.

And I caught myself thinking, what would I do without her?

Another thought followed, more dizzying.

How would I have managed this if she had not come to Cameroon with me?

I had no answer.

So I did the only thing I could do in that seat above the Atlantic.

I thanked God for her.

For her presence.

For her strength.

For her loyalty.

For her capacity to carry what I could no longer carry.

In Atlanta, the lines moved. Security. Gates. The last flight.

When we arrived in Asheville, we collected our bags. Kristianna did not have Wi-Fi to order an Uber. She asked me to wait. She walked outside. I sat, exhausted, trusting that it would be okay.

A few minutes later, she came back with an Uber already arranged, ready to help me into the car.

Only later did she tell me what she had done. She walked to the pick-up area, found a driver, negotiated, explained the situation, set everything up without telling me so I would not have to make one more effort.

A simple gesture.

And for me, the size of the world.

A gesture that said, I see you. I understand. I am here.

And inside that gesture was something I had denied for years.

The need to be carried in return.

A need I had buried under performance and endurance.

That ride home was quiet. And it reminded me of a truth my body had been trying to scream for a long time.

Love is not proven only by carrying others.

Love is also proven by accepting to be carried.

SECTION XIV — RETURNING TO AN UNFAMILIAR BODY

When we arrived, I collapsed onto the couch.

And the words came out of my mouth like reflex.

Home sweet home.

Not a caption. Not a punchline.

An exhale.

From the outside, the trajectory looked clear. I survived the stroke. I left the hospital. I endured the tensions. I crossed airports. I made it home.

So everything should be better.

But inwardly, it did not move in a straight line.

The first minutes on that couch were silent. Kristianna moved gently around me, putting away a few things, checking practical details.

I stared at the ceiling. Then the wall. Then my right hand.

Everything in the room was familiar. The living room. The couch. The light through the window. The smell of the house.

And yet something was wrong.

I felt an odd heaviness, as if my body did not fully belong to me anymore. My movements were slowed. My thinking thickened. My emotions felt raw.

I was not only tired.

I was foreign to myself.

That is when I understood, dimly, that the most difficult return would not be the route from Yaoundé to Addis, Frankfurt, Atlanta, and Asheville.

The longest return would be the one back to my own body.

The conflict–illness dynamic changed shape again.

After the acute and visible crisis, another struggle began. Living with a body that no longer obeyed. Living with emotions that overflowed. Living with an identity that no longer fit the old roles.

The inner storm did not come with sirens.

It installed itself quietly in ordinary life.

The fear of spilling a drink.

The hesitation before speaking on the phone.

The sudden fatigue after a short walk.

The need to lie down in the middle of the day.

The way my eyes avoided the mirror.

My body had forced my life to stop. Now my inner world had to catch up.

And at the center of it all, a question began to follow me.

What happens inside me when I can no longer be the man I have always shown the world?

I did not yet have the language of theory.

I had the sensation.

I am living in an unfamiliar body.

I am inhabiting a life that resembles mine without fully belonging to me.

CONCLUSION — THE STORM RELOCATES

This chapter ends on that couch in Asheville, with that exhale.

Home sweet home.

From the outside, it looks like the storm is over.

But healing does not erase the storm.

It relocates it.

It makes it more subtle, more intimate, more demanding.

It moves conflict into personal places.

Self-worth.

Faith.

Marriage.

The way I see myself as a man.

As a husband.

As a son.

As a professional.

And here the conflict–illness framework gains another dimension. It is not only the conflict that precedes illness. It is not only the conflict that erupts during the acute crisis.

It is also the conflict that accompanies recovery itself.

Because very soon, another truth will impose itself.

Progress will not be linear.

Good days will live beside setbacks.

Encouragement will mingle with frustration.

Other people's you look fine will collide with my nights of anxiety.

This is the paradox I was about to enter.

Deep gratitude to be alive.

Deep destabilization at what this new life required.

I did not know the name of that paradox yet.

I only knew that I had survived the outer storm.

And now, inside the quiet of my own living room, the inner storm was beginning.

PART II

THE HIDDEN WAR OF RECOVERY

4

THE RECOVERY PARADOX

When I collapsed onto the big living room couch and murmured, "Home sweet home," I still did not know that this sigh marked the beginning of a new season. The acute storm had passed: the stroke in Cameroon, the clinic, the ISIS hotel, the flights, the airports, the return inside a body I no longer recognized.

But that night in Asheville, something else began:

the long crossing of healing.

And very quickly, I discovered a truth I never imagined I would one day write:

I did not go through this season of my life alone.

I could not have.

The road of recovery revealed something fundamental to me, something neither my studies, nor my work, nor my pride as an independent man had managed to teach me: we never heal in solitude. Real healing, the kind that demands you rebuild yourself from the inside, requires witnesses, support, outstretched hands, quiet presences that remind you that life has not given up on you.

I often think of all the people who prayed, sent a message, prepared a meal, offered a word of encouragement, or simply kept a place for me in their hearts while I was learning to breathe differently, to walk differently, to live differently. I will never be able to thank each of them properly. Words are too short when it comes to deep gratitude. They run out of breath in front of the tenderness of what I received. And yet every name, every gesture, every look matters. Together, they formed an invisible net that kept me from falling even lower.

But there is one person for whom words will always be insufficient: Kristianna.

How do you thank someone who carried you when you no longer had strength?

How do you express the gratitude you feel toward the one who constantly pushed her own limits to protect yours?

How do you put language to the faithfulness of a woman who watched over your breath the way one watches over a fragile flame in the wind?

No sentence, no chapter, no book will be enough.

There is no vocabulary wide enough to say what her courage, her patience, and her love have meant to me.

I know only this: without her, I might not be writing these lines.

The road of recovery forced me to learn something difficult: dependence.

I had built my life on autonomy, on handling things, holding it down, staying upright no matter what, and I had to learn to be carried. I had to accept help beyond what my pride could tolerate. I had to recognize that I could not control everything: not my body, not my emotions, not even my thoughts.

That forced dependence shook something deep inside me. It made me vulnerable in a new way, almost disorienting. It forced me to meet myself the way you meet a stranger.

Because in fragility, you often discover a part of yourself you did not know, or a part you had avoided your whole life.

I thought I knew myself. I thought I understood what drove me, my motivations, my wounds, my convictions. But illness brought to light areas I had never dared to look at too closely: my fear of disappointing, my need to prove myself, my difficulty slowing down, my tendency to absorb more than my body could carry.

It also revealed, with an honest brutality, that I had been living with silent tensions for a long time, tensions accumulated beneath responsibilities, expectations, and the weight of roles I had learned to play. My body had become the messenger, and the stroke its loudest cry.

The recovery paradox begins here.

Recovery is the strange season in which survival brings gratitude to the surface while disorientation continues its work underneath.

On one side, I was infinitely grateful to be alive. On the other, I had to live with a body moving according to a logic that was no longer mine.

Before the stroke, I believed progress was linear. I believed work, discipline, and willpower were enough to move forward. I believed effort could repair almost anything.

But recovery makes a mockery of our old certainties.

It follows no plan.

It honors no urgency.

It does not cooperate with our schedules.

It moves like a tide: one step forward, two steps back. Then one day, without warning, a tiny gesture becomes a victory, a breath becomes a promise, a quiet night becomes a miracle.

Recovery taught me humility. It taught me patience. It taught me that the body never lies, and that it always ends up demanding what the mind has ignored for too long. It also taught me that the presence of others is sometimes the only strength that keeps us standing.

And it is at the heart of this tension, between gratitude and frustration, hope and exhaustion, thanksgiving and disorientation, that the Recovery Paradox truly begins.

To understand it, I must return to the first days.

SECTION I — THE FIRST DAYS

The first days in Asheville had the texture of apprenticeship. Not a spectacular apprenticeship, not the kind we associate with a degree or visible success. It was quiet, almost fragile: learning to live again.

And in that school, Kristianna was the pillar, the teacher, the guardian of day and night.

When we finally arrived in Asheville that night, after more than a month away from home, I felt a relief in her so deep it looked like muscles letting go. We were back. But being home did not mean life instantly found its rhythm again. She knew the situation demanded a sudden shift, the ability to turn the page without transition. For a while, everything rested on her, and she carried that weight without ever naming it.

Me, I slept.

She stayed awake.

I would wake up very early, often between 6:00 and 6:30, after surprisingly good nights. I was so exhausted that sleep became therapeutic. For the first time in a long time, I was truly resting, as if my body had finally been given permission to collapse. I slept with my CPAP mask, a faithful companion through those nights of rebuilding.

The experience was not the same for her.

Months later, after Amarah was born, we came back to that period. She searched for a word to describe what she was living. She said, "very stressful." I know now that this word was shorthand, a kind of modesty.

She asked me to imagine our sleep since Amarah's birth, how we react to the slightest sound, the smallest breath, the tiniest movement. Then she told me:

"My experience during your recovery was that, but much more intense. I knew you were not well. I knew at any moment something unexpected could send us to the ER. I had to be ready for anything."

Every time I got up to use the bathroom, she was already awake. She often repeated how disoriented I looked, confused, especially in the first weeks. That confusion returned regularly throughout the entire first year. She always took the time to speak to me gently, to anchor me, to remind me where I was.

Some nights, she would shake me to tell me my CPAP mask had stopped. Other times, she listened to me talk in my sleep, as if I were negotiating something in a dream, or trying to flee a shadow. She told me I would sometimes get up and take a few steps, incomprehensible phrases slipping out of my mouth.

I could not believe my nights were so restless.

I slept.

She kept watch.

Every morning, after I woke up, she took my blood pressure religiously. For six months, until the day I could finally do it myself. After our first medical appointment, the doctor prescribed a device to measure my blood sugar. Once again, she handled it, every morning, without fail.

Then came the first meal of the day: a bowl of sugar free yogurt, always prepared with the same care. She added strawberries, blueberries, blackberries, oats, walnuts, almonds, chia, and flax. A simple meal, designed to support a tired and vulnerable body. I never felt heavy, only held.

At lunch, she made me eggs, sometimes scrambled, sometimes whole, with herbs, broccoli, ham, salami, or sujuk. Always something nourishing, always something that made me feel as if I was finding my footing again.

At night, she made sure I ate between 7:00 and 8:00. She had read, studied, researched everything that could help me reverse type 2 diabetes, regain my strength, and stabilize my weight. Each dinner followed the same pattern: a salad with tomatoes, avocado, and onions, dressed with lemon, olive oil, and salt. Then meat or fish with green beans or white beans. And always an apple cut into small pieces to finish.

I still cannot believe the discipline with which she made sure I ate those meals every evening for six months.

Before bed, around 9:30 or 10:00, she took my blood pressure and my glucose again. My blood pressure was so unstable that she sometimes called the on-call doctor, late, early, whenever she had to.

Fear was never spoken, but it lived in her hands.

That was our routine.

Our way of walking in the dark with a small lamp.

Our way of surviving.

Our way of hoping.

And it was within this frame, made of simple rituals, repeated gestures, silent vigils, that I began to understand recovery is not only medical.

It is relational.

It is embodied.

It is woven into the faithfulness of a fragile daily life.

SECTION II — THE FIRST ASSESSMENT

As much as I wanted to forget what had happened to me in Cameroon, August 2023 still carried the full weight of that journey. I had returned to Asheville, but I did not feel fully returned. My body seemed to hover between two continents, two realities, two versions of myself.

I thought I was not that bad physically, considering what I had just survived. But in my mind, nothing was clear.

In that state, I made an appointment almost immediately with my primary care physician.

I remember the way I walked into her office: slowly, with a new vigilance that no longer left me. I was walking, but without confidence. I did not know whether I had lost my balance or whether my mind simply no longer trusted my body. That sensation followed me for nearly a year.

Kristianna had prepared all the documents from Nkomkana, test results, reports, prescriptions. Everything was in French. And for the first time, I became fully aware of the gap between surviving an experience in one medical system and having to translate it into another.

She translated. She explained. She finished my sentences when they slipped away from me. The doctor listened, read, observed, without impatience, without judgment.

It was reassuring to feel that she was entering our story not as a distant technician, but as an attentive witness. She asked questions, clarified, stitched together the pieces of the puzzle between two healthcare systems. Slowly, a coherent picture emerged. She saw. She understood.

That alone brought immense relief.

She took my vitals, ordered a glucose test, evaluated each parameter with methodical attention. Her posture, her voice, her gaze created a space where, for the first time in weeks, my vigilance dropped a notch.

Then she said words that marked a turning point:

"I'm optimistic. You will recover. But it will take time. And you will need to be patient with yourself."

Something in me settled when she said that. She did not minimize. She did not dramatize. She located me.

She then established a schedule: weekly visits, close follow up, precise and structured. She recommended an outpatient rehabilitation program at Mission Hospital CarePartners, speech therapy, cognitive evaluation, physical support. She already had a plan, even though I had not yet fully recovered my words.

I left her office fragile, but less lost.

Fragile, but accompanied.

Healing, at this stage, did not begin with a miracle cure. It began with an encounter: someone who looks directly at your story and simply says,

"You are not alone here anymore. We will move forward together."

SECTION III — RELATIONSHIPS UNMASKED

After returning from Cameroon, I gradually began informing my colleagues and key people at work about what had happened to me. I wanted them to understand the reality of my situation, not to elicit pity, but so that necessary arrangements could be made.

Most responded with a kindness I will never forget. They sent short letters, simple but sincere messages wishing me a quick recovery. Some came to see me during the first weeks, then regularly throughout the first year. One colleague came early on to cut my hair. Others sat with me, sometimes in a silence that said more than any speech.

With a few of them, we walked. Short outings that, at the time, felt like real expeditions.

I did these walks at least three times a week. Kristianna often came with me. Before the stroke, I would have hesitated to even call this exercise. Afterward, every step became a conscious effort, a negotiation between my will and a still hesitant body.

For the first three months, walking felt almost insurmountable. I was short of breath in a new, unfamiliar way, as if my breath had been misplaced somewhere between Yaoundé and Asheville.

Certain walks remain vivid in my memory, especially those of the first two weeks with a colleague and friend. Everything happened in a fog. I struggled to line up words. Thoughts came, but the path between my brain and my mouth was congested. Sometimes I gave up speaking altogether. It frustrated me deeply. A quiet shame crept in:

Why would he want to walk with someone who could not even hold a conversation?

I caught myself imagining what this might mean for my professional future if things did not improve quickly.

What surfaced in those moments went beyond physical weakness. The stroke had exposed older tensions I had carried for years:

the distance between the strong man I had learned to be and the vulnerable man I had become

the gap between my need for autonomy and my new dependence

the fracture between the role I inhabited at work and the reality of a man now moving in small steps, exhausted, hesitant, sometimes unable to speak

Illness had cracked the boundary between inside and outside.

In every organization where I have worked, I used to run a small exercise, a kind of relational thermometer. One day, I would be the one who systematically greeted every adult I crossed paths with, counting how many I greeted. The next day, I counted how many greeted me spontaneously without prompting.

It was not scientific, but it was telling. It revealed something about climate, culture, reciprocity.

After the stroke, that exercise took on a different meaning. It was no longer just a professional tool. It became a way of measuring how my existence, slowed and fragile, was being perceived.

Before, it would hardly have affected me.

After, every missed glance felt like a small sting.

And every gesture of presence felt like a blessing.

Illness, in this sense, unmasks relationships. It acts as a revealer. It brings to light what was already there but hidden by the speed of life.

A colleague, in coordination with Kristianna, set up a form to organize rides to my medical appointments. She herself drove me during the first week. The wife of one of my colleagues, who was also Kristianna's supervisor, organized a meal train. For two weeks, friends and colleagues took turns preparing homemade food for us.

Being fed by others, literally, during a season when I was learning to depend had something sacred about it.

But there were also silences.

People who said nothing, wrote nothing, asked nothing.

Before, I would have rationalized: People are busy. It is not personal.

After, those absences carried a different weight.

Vulnerability changes the way silence lands. The response of others, whether warm or hesitant, whether present or absent, enters the healing process. It can soothe what is already tender or press more deeply into the fear of becoming a burden.

SECTION IV — DUKE AND THE ORDEAL OF WAITING

Even though only two weeks had passed since my return, my morale was holding up surprisingly well, at least as well as one could expect after surviving a stroke. I tried to honor each day with a form of gratitude, even if I still did not quite know how to inhabit this new body, this new reality. I was moving on unstable ground, but I was no longer in the absolute chaos of the first days. It felt like walking on a surface that still trembled but no longer collapsed beneath my feet.

My meeting with the Head of School had gone better than I expected. I struggled to express myself. Words crowded, collided, stumbled. At times I stuttered, searching for sentences the way one searches through an overturned box. And yet he welcomed me with respect and care. He listened all the way through, waited for me to finish, did not supply my words for me.

That simple exchange reminded me of something essential: even in seasons when you lose part of yourself, there remain spaces where you are still recognized. I was diminished, but I was not erased.

I knew, however, that the road ahead would be long. Administrative processes, medical follow ups, accommodations at work, everything stood in line, waiting. I had to begin somewhere.

So Kristianna scheduled an appointment at the Duke Stroke Center in Durham, North Carolina. A three-hour drive from Asheville. This time, the destination carried a very different weight. This was not a trip for a basketball game or a tournament. It was a journey meant to understand what my body had decided to do without consulting me.

Duke's neurology department is recognized as one of the best in the country. Just hearing the name gave the impression of drawing closer to reassuring expertise. But hope came at a cost: the first available appointment was nearly two months away.

Two months.

When you are living with a brain that has failed without warning, two months is not time. It is an eternity. Each day carries the shadow of a question:

Could it happen again?

Kristianna and I did not really know how to position ourselves. Should we wait? Push? Look for another option? Seek a second opinion? Nothing was clear.

The waiting did not produce only medical uncertainty. It awakened deeper uncertainty too. The unanswered questions about my body stirred unanswered questions about my whole way of living.

In moments like these, the line between legitimate fear and residual anxiety becomes very thin. Every decision feels overloaded. The body, still shaken, sends signals. The mind, tired, amplifies them. You find yourself caught in a confused dialogue between the physiological and the psychological, asking:

What is coming from my body?

What is coming from my history?

What belongs to the stroke, and what was already there, quietly, long before?

Here again, the recovery paradox revealed itself: we wait for medical answers, but what illness awakens is often far broader than a diagnosis.

SECTION V — THE NIGHT OF AUGUST 9

It was in this context that the night of Wednesday, August 9, 2023, arrived, a few days after a block party organized with colleagues to celebrate the end of summer. I had attended, still fragile but grateful to be there, placing one foot back into social life.

That evening had been ordinary on the surface. I had taken a nap late in the afternoon, which had become almost habitual since the stroke. My body was demanding rest the way one finally demands repayment of an old debt.

I woke up abruptly. Disoriented. My eyes were open, but my mind was still caught in a dense fog. A brief vertigo, or perhaps that strange moment when you realize you no longer inhabit your body the way you used to.

Kristianna panicked immediately. And I cannot fault her for that. One of the most repeated warnings about strokes is the risk of recurrence. For loved ones, that risk is not an abstract phrase. It is a sword hanging overhead. Every silence that lingers, every gaze that drifts, every hesitant movement becomes a potential alarm.

Without giving me time to gather myself, she administered the FAST test, the one nearly every stroke survivor's loved-one learns by heart: Face, Arms, Speech, Time. My stuttering, the confusion of waking, my fear layering itself onto hers, made the reading uncertain. I could see doubt attacking her from all sides.

For her, it was out of the question to gamble with my life.

The ambulance arrived quickly. Four or five firefighters filled the living room with precise gestures and repeated questions. They observed me, ran the test again, evaluated my face, my arms, my speech. They seemed reassured: my face, though already marked by the stroke, was not drooping further. My strength was symmetrical. I could respond, even slowly. Their calm contrasted sharply with the anxiety that had saturated the room minutes earlier.

Kristianna needed clear markers. She asked them directly:

"What exactly are the signs that should make me call emergency services?"

They answered patiently. They confirmed that she had done the right thing. They added that taking the ambulance was an option, but that it would be costly, and that it would be reasonable for us to drive ourselves to the emergency room.

I was not enthusiastic about returning to the hospital. The walls of medical units still carried the scent of anguish for me, of grave announcements, of helplessness.

But the real question was not what I wanted.

The real question was:

What does Kristianna need to breathe?

Recovery places demand on loved ones as much as on the patient. Ignoring her fear would have been another form of violence.

So she began packing a travel bag, grabbing whatever her hands found, t-shirt, underwear, a tracksuit. I was already wearing a black Nike outfit. That night was not about elegance. It was about simplicity, speed, and a certain surrender: accepting that I no longer controlled everything.

I could not drive. My brain had been shaken too deeply, my body too fragile. So Kristianna took the wheel. I remember the way she closed the car door, firm, but not abrupt. The gesture of someone who holds, who carries, who does not allow herself to collapse.

The street was nearly empty. The night felt dense, as if the air itself weighed more. Headlights carved pieces out of the darkness. In the car, there was that mix of silence and wordless prayer.

I do not remember talking much. What I remember most is a feeling of shift.

Something inside me was preparing itself.

Not for catastrophe, as I would later understand.

For a turning point.

SECTION VI — MISSION HOSPITAL

We arrived at the hospital between 7:30 and 8:00 p.m. The parking lot was nearly full. We circled for a while before finding a space. Even the walk to the emergency entrance was an ordeal. Every step required a new kind of concentration, a constant inner monitoring.

As soon as I entered, I was struck by the crowd. An overwhelming number of patients were waiting. Some sat in chairs. Others lay directly on the floor. Sheets were spread here and there, bodies curled up, faces drained. A few slept without blankets.

The scene immediately reminded me of hospitals in Cameroon: hallways filled with families, people lying on the ground hoping for a bed, slow ceiling fans, the overlapping sounds of conversation, sighs, crying.

I was not in Yaoundé or Douala.

But my body recognized something.

An old memory was waking up.

What I was seeing that night was not just an overcrowded waiting room. It stirred deeper interior landscapes: illness in my family, the healthcare system of my country of origin, the fragility of poor bodies, the normalization of suffering.

My stroke was no longer just an isolated medical event. It had begun to speak to an entire personal and collective history.

Registration itself went smoothly. They asked my name, my age, the reason for my visit. I struggled to align words, but Kristianna stepped in. She recounted the evening, explained the stroke, described what she had observed.

My blood pressure was taken: relatively stable. A reassuring sign. Then they ran another stroke assessment. I passed it, which meant I was not showing signs of a new stroke. They fastened an identification bracelet around my wrist.

That simple plastic click stayed with me. In a second, I became a number in an overwhelmed system. The contrast between intimate fear and impersonal medical logic was hard to swallow.

We were then sent back to the waiting room. We found two empty chairs. All around us, patients kept arriving in waves. Some groaned. Others remained silent, absorbed by their pain.

Time passed with a peculiar slowness.

Around 1:30 in the morning, they finally called my name.

First evaluation. They asked the familiar questions again: symptoms, history, timeline of the evening. They rechecked my vitals. My blood pressure had risen slightly, nothing explosive, but enough to keep things serious. They gave me aspirin and sent me back to the waiting room.

Later, I was taken for a CT scan. The hallway was cold, nearly silent. The machine waited, indifferent, ready to read what my brain still refused to say clearly.

The scan was quick.

I returned utterly exhausted, stunned by the accumulated fatigue and stress.

At that point, exhaustion was so deep that even anxiety lost some of its grip.

Between 4:30 and 5:00 a.m., a room finally opened. They kept me in the emergency department for hours because, once you have lived through a stroke, every new symptom becomes an immediate concern. They wanted to rule out the worst before moving forward.

For me, those hours revealed something else. Waiting in that bright, crowded hallway forced me to confront the tension between wanting to minimize everything and finally accepting how fragile I still was. I was not simply being processed.

I was being protected.

SECTION VII — LEARNING SLOWNESS

The room was not particularly large, but compared to what I had known in Cameroon, it was another world. A clean bed. Quiet machines. Adjustable lights. A form of material dignity.

From that moment on, the rhythm changed.

Nurses rotated in regularly to check my vitals: blood pressure, heart rate, oxygen saturation, temperature, glucose levels. They watched every number, every fluctuation.

I must admit: I ate well in the hospital. The food was nothing remarkable, but for a body starved for rest and nutrients, it felt almost like a feast.

For four nights, several nurses took turns. Each had her own way of entering the room, of speaking, of making sure everything was okay. Some asked questions with an almost familial warmth. Others with a professional gentleness that was equally comforting.

I was sent to different departments for a battery of stroke related tests. Today, I would be incapable of listing them precisely. I was too tired, too dazed to register every step.

What I do remember clearly is a physical assessment on the second or third day. I was asked to walk a certain distance, then repeat the same path with my eyes closed. The instructor evaluated my coordination, my balance, my ability to follow simple instructions.

I passed every exercise.

Part of me wanted to declare victory.

But I knew better.

My primary physician had been very clear: no gym, no intense physical effort, only walking, for six to nine months. My body had to learn a new pedagogy: the pedagogy of slowness.

For someone who had long lived in performance, this was an inner upheaval.

The old version of me wanted to catch up, to prove everything was fine, to return to normal as quickly as possible. But normal for me was never casual. For most of my adult life, I trained like an athlete, lifting heavy, pushing my limits, shaping a body that could carry the weight of my responsibilities and the unspoken weight of my history. Strength, for me, was never only physical. It was symbolic. It was one of the ways I held myself together when life grew demanding or uncertain.

To go from that life of bench press, squats, deadlifts, long workouts, and a massive frame people recognized instantly, to slow walks around the neighborhood was devastating. I had never known a season in which I was forbidden to push, forbidden to lift, forbidden even to test myself. Being told to walk only, for six to nine months, felt like an exile from the world I had spent years building. For someone who shaped his identity around endurance, discipline, and a certain physical presence, this was not just a medical restriction. It was a profound personal loss.

I grieved quietly. I watched my muscles soften, my strength fade, and a body I had forged with discipline begin to feel unfamiliar. There were mornings when I looked in the mirror and did not recognize the man staring back. Beneath that physical grief lived a deeper truth: my former way of living, powered by performance, speed, and silent overextension, had helped create the very conditions that broke me down. My body had been telling the truth long before my mind was willing to listen.

Here, the collision became impossible to ignore. The strong, unshakeable man I had carried for years was meeting the fragile reality of healing. The old script insisted, “Push harder.” The new reality asked something very different: honor slowness, accept limits, choose gentleness over ego, and trust that your worth was never meant to rest on the weight of a barbell or the size of your frame.

Learning not to move faster than healing itself was not simply a medical adjustment. It was a spiritual one. It forced me to meet myself without the armor I had worn for decades, without the body I once relied on to hide my exhaustion, my fear, or my grief. And in that unguarded space, I began to understand that strength rooted in truth is nothing like strength rooted in performance. One demands relentless effort. The other invites honesty, humility, and a return to the kind of wholeness no mirror can fully reflect.

On the third or fourth day, several doctors came in to share the first results. They confirmed what had happened in Yaoundé: yes, it had been a stroke. No, the exact cause was not yet clearly identified. Hearing that confirmation so far from home carried its own weight. A part of me, small, quiet, but stubborn, had held on to the tiniest hope that the Cameroonian diagnosis might have been wrong. I knew the chances were slim, almost nonexistent, but hope has a way of clinging to improbable possibilities when we are afraid.

But in that quiet hospital room in Asheville, under the calm authority of doctors who had no reason to exaggerate or soften the truth, that fragile hope dissolved. There was no denying it. The stroke was real, and the impact on my body and mind was real. Accepting that truth felt like a second blow, one that required not emergency care, but humility.

Their next words steadied me. The prognosis was relatively good. They expected me to make a full recovery. Relief and fear braided together inside me, gratitude for the possibility of healing intertwined with the sobering reality that my body had spoken loudly, clearly, and without permission.

Their reassurance mattered, but it also demanded something of me. It asked me to release the last remnants of denial and to participate honestly in the long, patient work ahead. Recovery would not simply happen to me. I would have to meet it with truth, vulnerability, and a willingness to listen, finally, to what my body had been trying to tell me.

Kristianna was there throughout those days, a steady presence. She asked doctors questions. She took notes. She made sure nothing slipped through the cracks.

I do not remember all her questions or all the answers. I remember only this feeling: it is extraordinary to have her by my side.

On the fourth day, late in the afternoon, I was transferred to a larger private room, quiet, with a television, a small sofa, a private bathroom, and, strikingly, water readily available without complication.

I spent two more nights there.

It was neither a hotel nor a spiritual retreat. But for the first time in a long while, my body had a place to settle without urgency. I could be silent without having to justify it. I could sleep without feeling guilty for being unproductive.

Kristianna slept on the sofa. She was attentive to every detail.

I was discharged on August 15, 2023.

I did not feel like before.

But I felt alive in a different way.

There was a new kind of peace inside me, fragile, yes, but real. As if, in the back and forth between fear and care, between inner strain and medical accompaniment, something had begun to reconcile within me.

SECTION VIII — THE TEMPTATION TO MINIMIZE

Unfortunately, the story did not end there.

After a few days back at home, another night arrived to test how fragile our new sense of peace really was. On August 18, I had a nightmare. I woke up confused, disoriented, with that unpleasant sensation of being both present and absent at the same time.

For me, it was just a bad dream.

For Kristianna, it was a possible warning sign.

Once again, we found ourselves at Mission Hospital.

There was something disorienting about returning to the same place so soon, as if the threshold we had just crossed had quietly pulled us back. Some of the nurses at intake and triage recognized us. For them, we were faces among many. For us, they were the same witnesses accompanying a renewed fear.

I must be honest: I went reluctantly. Part of me thought Kristianna was reacting too strongly, driven by emotion. But how could I blame her? She was carrying the invisible weight of constant vigilance. When someone you love has had a stroke, peace becomes provisional. Every night carries a question mark.

At the hospital, the FAST test went well. My vitals were stable. I waited through the night until morning, when I was admitted for observation.

Waiting, during the first visit and the second, felt like a form of gentle torture: sitting for hours under artificial light, tense, not knowing when you will be called or what you will be told.

By the end, my body ached everywhere.

When they finally admitted me, shortly before 10:00 in the morning, it felt like a release. They ran more tests and kept me under observation through the day and into the night. They wanted to be sure nothing had been overlooked before I went home. By the next day, they allowed us to leave.

I did not yet fully understand it, but these repeated trips to the hospital marked a turning point. They forced me to take more seriously what my body was trying to say. They also exposed another tension: the pull to minimize, it is nothing, it will pass, and the reality of an organism permanently marked by a serious event.

The struggle was no longer hidden. It lived between minimization and lucidity, between the reflex of not wanting to bother anyone and the necessity of asking for help.

CONCLUSION — THE INNER ROOM

When we left the hospital that second time, something had shifted.

The fear of dying was still there, but it had moved to the back row. What pressed on me now was the question of how to live in a body I no longer trusted.

I could see more clearly the limits of my body, the hesitations in my speech, the fatigue of my mind. I could also see more clearly the weight all of this placed on Kristianna.

At the same time, the circle of support began to tighten gently. Messages came less frequently. Visits spaced out. Other people's lives resumed their normal rhythm.

This is not a moral failure. It is the natural order of things. No one can remain indefinitely suspended in the crisis of another.

But for the one who remains inside the healing process, something more subtle begins to take shape: a new kind of solitude.

Not the dramatic solitude of abandonment.

An inner solitude.

You are surrounded but not always understood.

You are alive, but not fully back.

You resume certain habits, but you are no longer the same person who built them.

At this stage, everything becomes quieter on the outside and more intense on the inside.

I had to learn how to live with a brain that worked differently, a mouth that sometimes hesitated, a memory that frayed at the edges. I had to continue functioning in a community where, gradually, people looked at me again as if everything were better, while inside, so much remained fragile.

This tension is where the next part of my story unfolds.

It is no longer primarily about emergency rooms, CT scans, or blood pressure readings. It is about speech therapy rooms where words do not come the way they used to. About fine rehabilitation exercises where progress is measured in millimeters, not milestones.

It is about the visit of Kristianna's mother, who came from Germany and saw me more fragile than she had ever known me to be. About what it means to be seen, loved, and sometimes worried over by another generation.

It is about my first major trip after the stroke, a wedding in Arizona, and the realization that even under an immense sky, one can feel constricted on the inside.

For now, I close this chapter with one conviction:

Healing is not only a matter of numbers and test results.

It is a story of relationships, of inner fractures laid bare, of bodies that speak when the soul falls silent, of grace received through ordinary gestures.

It is also the story of a new solitude, not one that says you are abandoned, but one that whispers:

You are becoming someone you do not yet know.

This is the solitude that will shape the next chapter.

5

A NEW FORM OF SOLITUDE

When Recovery Becomes Quiet and the Interior Conflict Begins

I never imagined discovering solitude precisely at the moment when the body finally speaks because you refused to listen earlier. During the crisis, everything had been unmistakably loud. There was the raw fear, the urgency, the prayers whispered and shouted, the hospital corridors, the medical language, the signs that something serious was unfolding. Once home in Asheville, there were the walks, the meals left at our door, the phone calls, the messages, the hands resting gently on my shoulder.

But then something shifted.

Not during the emergency.

Not during the return.

After.

Doctors speak of recovery. Loved ones speak of progress. Institutions speak of return. And yet, inside, the truth is not that clean.

The illness had delivered a clear message to my body. In Chapter 2, I described the moment when the body becomes a messenger, when it speaks because you refused to listen earlier. In Chapter 3, I wrote about the inner storm, the silent battle in which faith, memory, confidence, and identity all tremble at once. In Chapter 4, I tried to name the paradox of recovery, being surrounded while profoundly dependent, being supported while forced to reconstruct from within.

What appears next is harder to recognize. It emerges when the noise fades, when visits become less frequent, when life around you resumes its rhythm, when people begin to say with sincere relief, "You look better."

What emerges then is a solitude that did not exist before the illness. A solitude born from the distance between what others see and what you are still living on the inside.

People watch you walk.

They hear you speak.

They see you smile, joke, dress almost like before.

And they conclude, with the best intentions, "You're doing well."

Meanwhile, inside, you are still negotiating with the fear of recurrence, with waves of exhaustion that arrive without warning, with mental fog that disrupts the simplest tasks, with a hoarse voice you no longer recognize, with a body that has changed the way it carries you, with an identity that no longer fits its former anchors.

It was there that my understanding of illness deepened.

Before the stroke, I had mainly understood conflict as the relationship between unresolved inner tensions and the emergence of physical symptoms. But once illness strikes, another conflict appears.

A conflict that unfolds after survival.

Between the former self and the self that follows.

Between what others believe they are witnessing and what you are enduring.

Between the image of the comeback and reality.

This chapter follows that conflict as it unfolds. It moves through visits, meals, trips, and moments of joy that should, in theory, dissolve loneliness. And yet they revealed something else.

One can be deeply loved, sincerely supported, objectively privileged, and still feel displaced, as if no one can fully enter the space where the fracture has settled.

What follows is not an argument.

It is not a diagnosis.

It is a series of lived scenes.

Each one traces how this new form of solitude took shape, day after day, beginning on August 20, 2023, when the crisis had quieted, the body had stabilized, and the real interior work began.

SECTION I — BIMBO'S VISIT

On August 19, I had barely returned home. I had been discharged on August 15, and then, on August 19, fear pulled us back to the emergency room for another long night of vigilance. So when morning came and I found myself once more in our living room in Asheville, the relief was real, but it was not clean.

My body was stable, yet my nervous system still behaved as if the alarm had never fully stopped ringing.

Fatigue clung to my bones like a second skin. It was not the kind of tiredness sleep can resolve. It felt structural, as though my body had learned a new way of being weighed down.

That day, Kristianna received a call. It was Bimbo, as he is known in Cameroon, a longtime friend and someone I look up to, a former Cameroonian basketball player now living in Atlanta. He wanted to confirm our address. He planned to stop by the next day, August 20, around noon.

When she told me, something stirred inside me. Not a surge of energy. More like a small ember that refused to go out.

My mind went back to June, to the former players and teammates who had crossed entire states to attend my graduation from Nova Southeastern University in Florida. Three days of collective celebration, punctuated by Cameroonian songs and improvised dances that drew curious looks from passersby.

We were not performing.

We were reuniting.

The Cameroonian diaspora has a singular way of turning nostalgia into celebration, distance into fraternity.

Those memories kept me warm. They reminded me that before the illness had folded me inward, I had belonged to something rare and that I still mattered to that community.

The next day, when Bimbo stepped into the house, I felt my chest tighten. Not with pain, but with that strange vulnerability that settles after a shock, the awareness that someone is entering an intimate space and encountering a version of you that is no longer recognizable, even to yourself.

We would have liked to welcome him differently. With a rested face. A steady voice. A body that did not betray the recent battle it had survived.

Illness had opened a quiet but profound conflict within me: the gap between the man I still was for others and the man I had become.

Kristianna, faithful to her Middle Eastern culture, served him tea, dates, and nuts after lunch. Her gentleness filled the room. She listened attentively, asked questions, and guided the conversation with care.

I watched her and thought that even in my weakened state, I was rich in her presence.

We spoke about work, stability, privilege. I told him what my supervisor had said, that my only responsibility for now was to heal.

That word troubled me.

Heal sounded like a destination. Inside me, the road still felt foggy.

We spoke of Bofia's wedding, which had taken place while I was in crisis. He described the laughter, the dancing, the warmth of the moment. I told him my silence had not been indifference. I had been in a battle with the stroke at that very time.

Illness creates a mute fracture. You continue to love people, but you become hesitant, unsure how to remain present in their lives.

He stayed for three hours.

At one point, I noticed in the way he was watching me that he understood. My energy was dispersing. My voice grew heavy. My shoulders began to slump.

With the kind of delicacy that reveals genuine friendship, he apologized politely and stood to leave. Before he did, he embraced me.

I had never felt so small.

Not a humiliating smallness.

A truthful one.

I was a vulnerable man, unsteady, physically diminished. In a matter of weeks, I had gone from a size 3XL to a size L. But the most brutal change was not in the clothes.

It was in the way I perceived myself.

Illness had performed an interior contraction, a shrinking of certainties, of illusions of control, of that visible and recognized presence that had long been my signature.

Solitude begins before it is named.

It begins when the external world resumes its rhythm while your inner world remains under construction.

Bimbo's visit reminded me of something essential.

One can be surrounded, loved, supported, and still feel an inner emptiness no one else can fill.

Illness does not only tear you away from routines.

It tears you away from a version of yourself.

And the road toward finding a new place in one's body, one's life, one's identity is a perilous path that must, at least in part, be walked alone.

SECTION II — THE HOUSE FILLS, THE INTERIOR EMPTIES

The days that followed Bimbo's visit unfolded with a strange duality. The house was not empty. People were calling, checking in, offering prayers and encouragement. Some came by briefly. Others stayed longer, sitting with me in that careful way people adopt when they sense fragility but do not know how to name it. And yet, beneath this activity, something in me continued to withdraw.

It was not withdrawal born of bitterness or resentment. It was quieter than that, more confusing. A kind of internal retreat that happened without conscious decision, as though my body and mind had agreed, without consulting me, that this was a season for inward movement.

My identity had been relational and outward facing. I thrived on interaction, on presence, on the energy that comes from being needed and recognized. Leadership, teaching, coaching, mentoring, each role fed that orientation. I had learned to inhabit rooms fully, to read people quickly, to offer strength as if it were an unlimited resource.

But now, something had shifted.

Conversations required effort.

Laughter demanded energy.

Listening exhausted me.

I found myself nodding, smiling, participating just enough to reassure others, and perhaps myself, that I was still there. But after each interaction, a wave of fatigue followed, deeper than physical tiredness. It felt as though every exchange drew from a reserve that had not yet been replenished.

This was the aftermath of a conflict that had long lived quietly inside me. I had absorbed tensions, professional, relational, spiritual, without allowing myself to register their weight. The stroke had interrupted that pattern abruptly. Recovery was now forcing me to reckon with the consequences.

What surprised me most was how little this experience could be shared.

When someone asks, "How are you feeling?" the socially acceptable answer after a medical crisis is simple: "Better." It reassures the listener. It signals progress. It allows life to move forward.

But better is an imprecise word.

Better than the ICU. Yes.

Better than the fear of not surviving. Without question.

But better does not mean whole.

And there was no easy way to explain that to people who loved me. How do you articulate an absence? How do you name a solitude that exists even in company? I did not have the language yet. All I had was the sensation, a persistent feeling of being slightly out of sync with the world around me.

The house could be full.

The calendar could contain appointments.

The phone could buzz with messages.

And still, inside, there was a quiet space that remained untouched.

Support does not automatically translate into understanding. People can walk beside you without entering the terrain you are navigating. Not because they do not care, but because some landscapes are inaccessible to those who have not crossed them.

I began to recognize that my solitude was not a failure of community. It was part of transformation.

Transformation isolates before it integrates. Before something new can be inhabited, the old structures must loosen their grip. The roles I had once relied on, leader, problem solver, caretaker, were no longer sufficient. But the new configuration of self had not yet taken shape. I was suspended between identities, between capacities, between narratives.

This suspension carried its own form of loneliness.

And yet, within that loneliness, something else was quietly unfolding, an invitation to listen more closely, not to the expectations around me, but to the signals within. My body, which had already forced the first interruption, continued to communicate through fatigue, through silence, through a resistance to perform normalcy too quickly.

The conflict was no longer only about illness.

It was about permission.

Permission to be unfinished.

Permission to be less available.

Permission to exist without immediately being useful.

That permission did not come easily. It challenged the very foundations on which I had built my sense of worth. But it was becoming unavoidable.

Recovery, I was learning, is not simply the return to life as it was.

It is the negotiation of a new relationship with oneself.

And that negotiation, by its very nature, unfolds in solitude.

SECTION III — THE VISIT FROM GERMANY

There are presences that do not enter a home so much as they settle into it. They do not impose themselves. They alter the air quietly. Kristianna's mother belongs to that rare category of presence. When she arrived from Germany, I was still in that fragile zone where the body appears to have returned, but the interior self continues to stumble. Recovery was already underway, at least by external standards, yet I felt no sense of arrival. Only a careful balancing.

She came without fanfare. No dramatic gestures. No excessive questions. She moved through our house as if she were part of it, as if she had always been there. She respected each room, each silence, each pause. She tidied without noise. She observed without staring. She lived among us without displacing anything.

Very quickly, she claimed the small patio behind the house as her refuge. She would go there to smoke a cigarette, read a book, or call Germany. Her voice was often low, almost whispered, as though she were protecting the morning itself. Sometimes she laughed softly. Sometimes she sat in silence with someone on the other side of the world. Even when she was outside, her presence stabilized the house. It was as if an additional layer of calm had been laid over our daily rhythms.

And then there was her cooking.

I place her easily in the top three cooks I have ever known. When she was with us, I ate without restraint. Her food carried a warmth that defied translation. It was not merely good. It was sustaining. Some mornings she prepared shakshuka, the pan still crackling, the smell of tomatoes, peppers, and soft spices filling the house before I reached the stairs. Other days, she made dolma, the Armenian grape leaf version, tightly rolled, fragrant with garlic, mint, and slow-cooked rice, each one assembled with a precision that felt almost maternal. She made many other dishes too, meals shaped by the flavors of her own story, dishes that filled the house with a tender Middle Eastern aroma I already knew from Kristianna's cooking and trusted right away because she had cooked for me year after year. It was as if each plate carried something she could not express in English, something of her care for Kristianna, something of her concern for me. Food became a form of language, one she spoke fluently and generously.

She herself had much to manage. Responsibilities in Germany. Administrative obligations that followed her even across borders. And yet she did not hesitate to come. She recognized, perhaps before I fully did, that Kristianna was carrying an enormous weight. She came not to replace her, but to help bear that load quietly, without announcement.

What astonished me most was that we did not share a spoken language.

She did not speak English.

I did not speak German.

She was almost always awake before I was. I would come downstairs slowly, still wrapped in fatigue, still surprised by the heaviness that greeted me each morning. And she would be there, seated, present, available. Not waiting in the sense of anticipation, but available in the sense of openness.

We communicated through our phones, translated questions, careful responses, small comments that made us smile. I could take my time. I never felt rushed. I never sensed impatience. She spoke to me as if nothing else demanded her attention.

That kind of presence unsettled me in the best way.

Without knowing it, she became a witness.

Not because she understood everything.

Not because she knew what I was enduring.

But because her presence demanded nothing from me.

She did not need clarity.

She did not require performance.

She did not ask me to narrate my experience in ways that would make sense to her.

With her, I could exist without effort.

She did not remove my solitude, but she made it less threatening. She allowed it to breathe. I could be slow without embarrassment. Fragile without apology. Silent without discomfort. And in that space, something in me softened.

At the same time, her presence illuminated another tension, one I had been avoiding.

How do you allow your spouse into your darkest days when those days are many?

How do you ask for support without becoming a burden?

How do you remain close when you no longer have the language to describe what hurts?

Watching Kristianna interact with her mother brought these questions to the surface. I knew how much my wife was already carrying. I feared adding weight to a load she was bearing with extraordinary grace. This fear of needing too much sat at the center of my solitude.

Illness does not only affect the individual body. It reorganizes relationships. It reshapes intimacy. It introduces new silences into spaces once filled with ease.

When her mother eventually left, the absence was sharper than I expected. The house lost a particular calm, a specific gentleness. Before she went, I asked when she thought she might return. She smiled softly and, through the mediation of a phone screen, said, "The time will come. For now, think of yourself. Think of Kristianna. Build your family. That work is done by two, without outside interference."

She had accompanied me to a certain point. The rest of the journey belonged to Kristianna and me.

When the door closed behind her, I understood something essential. Even surrounded by love, certain spaces of recovery remain solitary. Not desperate. Not tragic. But necessary.

Her visit had been a grace.

Her presence, a balm.

Her departure, a summons.

A summons toward the next stage of recovery, where help recedes, and love must learn new forms of presence.

SECTION IV — THE MIRROR THAT SHOCKED ME

I do not think anyone truly prepares a patient for this moment, the moment when the body presents the bill for what it has endured. This reckoning does not arrive at the height of the crisis, nor during the first breaths of relief. It waits. It waits until you are walking a little straighter, until people begin to say, "You look better," until you dare to believe that the worst might be behind you. Then it arrives, not violently, but precisely, through something ordinary, a mirror, a recording, a reflection.

On the morning of September 4, Kristianna suggested an exercise she thought would be simple. She asked me to record my voice every day. Her intention was loving and strategic. She wanted to help me rebuild confidence, to recover an inner reference point that the illness had destabilized. She asked me to write a short introductory script, something professional, familiar, stable. She sensed that the stroke had not merely affected my speech. It had unsettled the place where my voice drew its authority.

I focused carefully.

"My name is Radar Onguetou.

I am the Director of Community Engagement, Diversity, and Belonging at Asheville School.

I consider myself patient and engaging.

I am here to talk to you about conflict resolution."

I placed my phone on the table, took a breath, recorded the video, and pressed play.

What came out of the screen cut through me like cold metal.

The voice I heard was not mine. Or rather, it belonged to a man I did not recognize. It lacked assurance. It lacked weight. It wavered slightly, as if each word were searching for balance. I stumbled over my own name. I tripped on Asheville School. The structure of the sentences was intact, but their soul was missing. My ear recognized the form, but my body rejected the sound.

Something in me knew immediately. Certain things were not going to return in the same way.

I listened again.

Once.

Twice.

Three times.

Each time, the same distance.

The same strangeness.

The same quiet shame.

A few days later, the mirror delivered the same message.

I was brushing my teeth when the light caught my face at an unfamiliar angle. My left cheek sagged slightly. My smile hesitated. My eye carried a fatigue that no amount of rest seemed able to repair. The asymmetry was subtle, so subtle that many would never have noticed. But I did.

My body stepped back before my mind could intervene.

Then I leaned in.

Something rose in me, fragile, painful, almost shameful. I had never feared mirrors. I had once loved photographs, perhaps too much. Images had documented my life, travels, games, friendships, beginnings in America. In 2004, I flooded my parents with photos as soon as I had access to a camera. I liked capturing life.

That morning, my reflection told no story.

It was an absence.

I recognized myself.

But I did not find myself.

This is where another layer of solitude begins, one invisible even to those who love you most. They see you walk. They hear you speak. They notice that you are almost yourself again. They celebrate your return. You want to celebrate with them. You want to believe that their love is enough to restore you.

But you know, deep down, that you have not yet come home.

On the outside, a functional man.

On the inside, a man searching for the fracture.

There was the Radar of before, confident, hurried, solid, accustomed to moving through the world without questioning his place.

And there was the Radar of after, slower, more vulnerable, more attuned to what silence conceals.

The mirror did not simply show asymmetry.

It exposed an identity rupture.

Those who love you can accompany you to its edge, but no further. They cannot hear your voice tremble through a screen. They cannot feel the moment your own face interrogates you.

Who are you now?

This was not tragedy. It was mourning, quiet and intimate.

I found myself avoiding photographs. Avoiding compliments about how good I looked. I pretended to believe them. But each reflective surface carried the same sting, the sense that I had left part of myself on a hospital table in Yaoundé, held between God, chance, and human limits.

Over time, I began to understand that this solitude was not punishment. It was invitation. The body, faithful messenger as it was, had revealed the wound long before the mind found language. And with each passing day, I sensed that this fracture was not an obstacle, but a doorway, an opening toward a truth I had never fully faced, the truth of a man learning again how to inhabit his own body.

Kristianna had given me a mirror I had never possessed before, not one of decline, but one of transition. There is a profound difference between being diminished and being vulnerable. Vulnerability opens a path. Diminishment closes it. She opened paths for me.

One morning, I listened again to the earliest recordings. Something shifted, not pride, but recognition. A quiet acknowledgment. Yes, I am fragile, but I am moving. Yes, I have stumbled, but I am standing again.

Perhaps Kristianna understood before I did. Healing is rarely spectacular. It is a sequence of small fidelities. A voice recorded each morning. A discreet proof that life had not been scattered. A trace I could revisit and tell myself, nothing is lost. Begin again.

SECTION V — THE TEST OF THE STEERING WHEEL

There are stages of recovery that cannot be anticipated, moments that appear insignificant from the outside but quietly redraw the internal boundaries of who you believe yourself to be. September 11 was one of those days. That Monday, Kristianna wanted to see whether I could drive again.

For her, it was an act of prudence, a reasonable step before asking the doctor for official clearance. For me, it was something else entirely. It felt like a summons. Not a test of coordination or memory, but a question posed to my inner coherence.

I knew I could drive. The mechanics were intact. The reflexes had not disappeared. But illness had introduced a new reality into my life. Competence no longer guaranteed confidence. I could technically complete this task, but I was unsure whether I was ready to carry what it symbolized.

Driving represented the return of autonomy, a longing that had burned quietly in me since my return to Asheville. To go out alone. To move without being monitored. To reclaim the simple dignity of choosing when and where to exist. And yet, alongside that desire lived another impulse, just as real, the fear that autonomy was arriving too soon.

This fear had nothing to do with ability. I knew I could react quickly enough. My energy was sufficient. Cognitively, I was steady. The struggle had nothing to do with skill. It had everything to do with what driving symbolized. In those weeks, I had become so dependent on Kristianna, almost hiding my insecurities behind her steadiness, that sitting behind the wheel meant standing without my shield. It meant having no place to hide the tremors that still lived beneath the surface.

Kristianna sensed the tension. Her voice remained gentle, encouraging, infused with that firm tenderness that had sustained my recovery.

"Baby, you've got this," she said, placing her hand on my shoulder.

"It's so important that you're able to do things on your own again."

For her, watching me drive meant relief, a sign that this season of constant vigilance might finally loosen its grip. For me, it opened a new internal battleground.

When I sat behind the wheel and closed the door, two opposing forces rose within me. One was determined, almost eager, the part of me that wanted proof the illness had not claimed the final word. The other, quieter and deeper, still craved support, still leaned toward the safety of being carried. These two selves were not arguing over a skill. They were negotiating a place. The steering wheel became their meeting table.

When I started the car, my body responded without hesitation. The movements were smooth. The road felt familiar. The street recognized me. And yet, beneath that ease, a weight lingered, a sadness I could not immediately name. It was not fear of an accident. It was the quiet grief of releasing a dependence that had protected me when everything else collapsed.

Independence, once synonymous with maturity and strength, suddenly resembled abandonment. Not abandonment by Kristianna, but the abandonment of that fragile part of myself that had found refuge in her steadiness. Taking the wheel felt like telling that part of me, you must now stand on your own, even though you are still trembling.

This is a solitude few people name. It is not born of neglect or lack of love. It emerges from transformation itself, from the moment when others celebrate progress while your inner world experiences separation.

They see the gesture mastered.

They see the milestone achieved.

They see normalcy returning.

They do not see the fracture, the space between the body that moves forward and the soul that hesitates. They cannot feel the emotional risk contained in a simple left turn. They cannot sense the quiet question pulsing beneath the surface. Can I really rely on myself again?

Kristianna gently reminded me to stay focused, perhaps thinking my attention was drifting from the road. She could not know that the real challenge was unfolding a few inches inside my chest. That battle was private.

As we drove back, she took out her phone to take a picture. My first instinct was resistance. She said something like, "This is really big," with sincere enthusiasm, even relief. She saw a milestone, a sign that the future was beginning to glow again.

In that photograph, I saw something else, the distance between who I had been and who I was becoming. Not a painful distance, but a real one. One I would have to learn to inhabit without shame.

That image became quiet evidence of a truth I was only beginning to grasp. Healing is not simply a return. It is a transformation. And transformation carries with it a solitude that no one else can bear for you.

SECTION VI — JERON'S VISIT

Some visits arrive like breath sent by God in moments of inner suffocation. They do not alter diagnoses or repair damage, but they bring a density of presence that eases what has been carried in silence. Jeron's visit was of that kind. He had written earlier in the evening to say he would arrive between 9:30 and 10:00 p.m.

I knew he had gently insisted on coming, not out of curiosity, but out of loyalty. He seemed willing to sit with me even if I was no longer fully upright within my own story.

Jeron is more than a friend. He entered my life at a formative moment, long before I understood the forces shaping me. We met in 2009, and from our earliest conversations, we recognized something rare in each other, softness beneath toughness, clarity beneath performance, soul beneath the athlete. We were both undersized power forwards, accustomed to compensating with willpower for what we lacked in inches. Knowing that he was arriving at the University of New Hampshire just as I was leaving created a strange bond, one of succession and continuity, as though our stories overlapped without colliding.

But what truly united us was not basketball success. It was what the game had taken from us and what it had revealed. We had been shaped by a brilliant coach, capable of dissecting an opposing offense with surgical precision. But that excellence came at a cost, little space for humanity. In that system, I became a professional pleaser, executing without protest, saying yes to everything, erasing emotion to maintain equilibrium.

The roots of what I would later understand were already there. Illness did not invent inner conflict. It exposed what had been quietly accumulating. I had learned to contain tension, minimize discomfort, and mute emotional signals in the name of performance. That conditioning strengthened my exterior but weakened my interior listening.

Jeron knew this. He had lived it too. We had spoken often about this silent pedagogy of endurance, the kind that teaches survival but neglects sensation. Our brotherhood deepened there, in the shared recognition of a fatigue that does not announce itself but understands.

When Jeron stepped through the door that night, it was nearly 11:00 p.m. I remember instinctively straightening my shoulders, a futile reflex meant to conceal what my body could no longer hide. I had lost weight. Lost some of my grounding. Lost the confidence with which I once occupied space. I wondered whether, behind his smile, he saw a diminished man or simply a friend who had reached his limit.

His gaze did not waver. He did not linger on my slowness or my altered posture. He greeted me as if I were intact. That simple act unsettled me more than any comment could have. It was as though he offered continuity at a moment when I could no longer locate it myself.

Still, a subtle shame surfaced, the shame of being seen in reduction by someone who had known me in strength. The shame of inhabiting a body I did not yet trust. The shame of measuring worth through physical presence. This fixation on stature and bearing was itself a symptom, the search for identity continuity, when identity fractures and the body clings desperately to visible markers that something of the former self remains.

He went to sleep quickly. I stayed awake long after. His presence under my roof awakened images of the man I had been, solid, quick, assured. I wondered whether that man would return, or whether I would need to learn to become someone else.

The next morning, we truly spoke. For the first time, I was able to tell the story without imploding. I did not recount every night in Yaoundé, every moment of pain and confusion, every hour in which I could not tell whether my body was abandoning me or fighting to keep me alive. I spoke instead of Kristianna, of her courage, her vigilance, the way she carried me when she had no space left to rest.

Jeron listened with an intensity that needed no response.

Then he told me about the first time he met Kristianna, in his apartment in Manchester. They had talked for hours, as two people do when they recognize depth without explanation. "I knew she would play an extraordinary role in your life," he said.

He spoke of our wedding at Lake Louise, the simplicity, the clarity, the silence of the mountains, the light on the water. Hearing that version of myself stirred something tender and painful at once. That Radar seemed aligned, grounded, whole. I wondered quietly whether he still existed.

A new solitude was taking shape. Returning to oneself was no longer automatic. It had to be reconstructed.

Before leaving, Jeron looked at me and said softly, "I don't know anyone stronger than you."

I smiled. But inside, a voice answered, if only you knew. I did not feel strong. I was standing, yes, but I was unsure what was holding me.

He saw courage I could not yet recognize. Kristianna saw it too. Perhaps the outside must sometimes name what the inside has forgotten.

When he left early that afternoon, the house filled with a distinct silence. Not emptiness. Density. The residue of a presence that does not fix everything but eases the burden of a man who believed he had to carry it alone.

On September 17, he sent a voice message. "Hey brother, I made it safely. Thanks again for having me. It's so good to see you. Gotta do it again sometime."

I listened to it several times. It was simple. Unadorned. And it said something essential. In this new solitude born of rupture and transition, some people know how to enter with reverence. They do not touch wounds. They do not diagnose. They do not force healing.

They enter.

They listen.

They recognize what you are carrying without claiming to understand it fully.

And sometimes, that is enough for recovery to breathe.

SECTION VII — THE FIRST OUTING WITH KRISTIANNA

On September 30, Bimbo returned to Asheville, this time with his wife. We agreed to meet at Capella on 9, a rooftop in downtown Asheville. On the surface, it was a simple evening out. For me, it was a quiet test, one that no one else could see. Could I still inhabit the world the way I once had?

I remember the moment Kristianna appeared in the living room before we left. She was radiant. Not simply beautiful, but regal in a way that carried dignity and endurance. She wore an azure, blue abaya, my favorite, its fabric flowing with an elegance that felt timeless. Her heels, her Persian earrings, everything about her presence reminded me of what she had carried in silence over the previous weeks.

A thought crossed my mind with unexpected clarity. I want to be worthy of her tonight.

But beneath that noble desire lay fear. Fear that my words would falter. Fear that the mental fog would return unannounced. Fear that I would be physically present but unable to follow the rhythm of a simple conversation. Fear, too, of not knowing how to inhabit this new body, this altered self, in public space.

Illness had not merely weakened me. It had shifted my internal coordinates. Each interaction now felt like a careful ascent, as if every word risked exposing the fracture between who I still appeared to be and who I was becoming.

I prepared topics in advance, literally. Like a student before a presentation. I was searching for anchors, something predictable that could hold me steady if my mind drifted. Improvisation, once second nature, now felt dangerous.

When I thanked Kristianna for everything, my words felt embarrassingly small compared to what she had borne. She had entered a season where everything depended on her, and she had done so without complaint. She carried it with a grace that exceeded me.

At Capella, we ordered drinks. Cocktails for them. Sparkling water for Kristianna. A Diet Coke for me. I had never been much of a drinker, even before the stroke.

We spoke of progress. Kristianna added details with her quiet pride. Laughter came easily enough. And yet, beneath the surface, I felt something suspended between us, a tension made of exhaustion and conversations postponed too long.

As the evening drew to a close, I noticed a shadow pass through her eyes. Barely perceptible. But I saw it. And immediately, a thought seized me. I ruined the evening.

A dull sadness settled in.

This, too, is part of post-illness solitude, reading too quickly, interpreting too deeply, feeling too much. This heightened sensitivity was not emotional weakness. It was the byproduct of an interior life still unsettled, an ongoing negotiation between outward normalcy and inner fragility.

I smiled.

I spoke.

I walked.

And yet I stood at the edge of a precipice no one else could see.

SECTION VIII — THE BROTHERS OF BASKETBALL

On October 20, the city filled with familiar accents, laughter, and shared memory. Djanabia arrived. Bofia and his wife joined him. Bimbo came again. They had rented an Airbnb not far from us.

We met at a café on Haywood Street, under a deceptive sun that shone without warming the air. When I saw them walk in, something in me exhaled. A quiet relief passed through my chest.

I had run into Djanabia during my official visit to the University of New Hampshire. I still remember the surprise of it. He had been lying on a couch in the locker room when I exclaimed, "Djanabia, is that really you?" We laughed, the kind of laughter that rises when coincidence reveals a deeper thread. I had known him long before America, back in Cameroon, where he was already a great basketball player and many youngsters like me hoped to reach the level he represented. Seeing him again, thousands of miles away, felt almost unreal. He guided me quietly during my time at UNH, making the transition less lonely. And Bofia, my contemporary, had always embodied a deep, steady solidarity, not only toward me, but toward all of us.

Once again, their presence made me feel small.

Not diminished.

Small in the way one feels when returning to a place where nothing needs to be proven.

Around that table, something in me relaxed. With them, I had no role to perform. No image to protect. No fear of disappointing anyone. No anxiety that walking would be mistaken for being healed.

They knew.

They understood even what I did not say.

African humor, direct, exaggerated, instinctively lucid, moved through me freely. I laughed without worrying about my lip drooping. I spoke without fearing that words would fracture. I paid attention, yes. I sometimes drooled without noticing. But I was not in surveillance mode.

I could say, "I still have more bad days than good," and know that no one would rush to interpret or minimize it.

With them, my fragility was not a subject for analysis.

It was welcomed.

Normal.

Human.

With them, I was myself, not the sick man, not the diminished man, not the fragile man. Just myself, with strength and fault lines intact. And for the first time in a long while, that was enough.

In that space, the split born of illness, between exterior normalcy and interior chaos, quieted. There were no longer two versions of me fighting for dominance. There was only one.

SECTION IX — THE SOCIAL MASK AND SHARED REPRIEVE

Later that afternoon, after resting with Kristianna, we joined them again at the Airbnb. I drove, a small triumph, a quiet confirmation that recovery was advancing, however modestly.

The warmth was immediate. Stories flowed. Jokes landed. Laughter moved through the room like lamplight, illuminating each face, each gesture, each shared memory.

At one point, as voices overlapped and joy filled the space, a thought struck me with surprising clarity. This is a final moment without masks.

Soon, we would return to our cities, our jobs, our obligations, our social identities. Each of us would put on again the version of ourselves the world expects. But here, in this living room, there was nothing to hide.

For me, it was more than comfort.

It was refuge.

Because I knew what awaited me afterward, the hardest stage yet, meeting myself again in solitude. Learning who I had become. Learning to inhabit a changed body. Learning to speak with a voice that hesitated. Learning to face a reflection that still startled me.

Post-illness solitude is not the absence of others.

It is the necessity of encountering oneself again, sometimes for the first time.

SECTION X — THE PALESTINIAN MEAL

For dinner that night at the Airbnb, still gathered with Djanabia, Bofia, and Bimbo, Kristianna suggested preparing a Palestinian dish, maqluba. It is not merely a meal. It is an act of patience and precision. Meat, chicken that day, layered with fried or roasted vegetables, then rice infused with spice, all assembled in a large pot. At first, I assumed it was an Armenian dish, since her mother is Armenian by birth and later naturalized German. Kristianna smiled and explained that it was Palestinian, one of those Levantine dishes shared across the region, adopted into Armenian homes through the long, quiet exchanges of culture and proximity. When cooked, the pot is flipped in one confident motion, revealing a savory cake, harmonious and abundant.

When she turned the pot and steam rose like an evening blessing, murmurs of satisfaction filled the room. The language of mmmh needs no translation.

We ate.

We laughed.

We gave thanks.

I watched Kristianna, the woman who had carried my life when I could not stand, and felt an urge rise in me to proclaim, this is my wife.

We stayed until 9:30 p.m. Time moved differently that night. It did not drag. It did not press. I tried to hold the moment close, knowing that the following day would return me to quieter, more fragile terrain.

Solitude after illness is like that. You savor the oases, fear the deserts, and keep walking. Because somewhere in that desert, God is shaping a new interior life, even when all you see is sand.

SECTION XI — THE WEDDING IN ARIZONA

Traveling again felt unreal, as though I were testing the limits of this new body, this altered self still searching for equilibrium. Peter, Patrick's younger brother, was getting married on November 4. Their family, Karen, Tim, and their sons, had played a formative role in my life. Despite fatigue and lingering fragility, I kept telling myself, you must go.

We traveled on November 3. As in so many stages of my recovery, Kristianna carried the invisible labor, medications, CPAP machine, water, logistics. She moved with a precision that felt like prayer. She was not only my partner. She had become my guardian.

The flight itself passed without incident. But upon arriving in Arizona, panic struck suddenly, the familiar fear of recurrence, the mental fog, the wave of exhaustion. I could not trace it to a specific trigger. It was the simple unease that settled into my body after sitting for so long, a heaviness that felt too close to the memory of what had happened in Cameroon. I realized then how deeply the trauma lived beneath the surface. Any sensation, any flicker of fatigue, any shift in my equilibrium, was immediately interpreted through the lens of the stroke. My body no longer trusted itself. And because of that, neither did my mind. Kristianna responded immediately. Uber. Directions. Airbnb. Her presence became my spine.

The apartment was simple, welcoming. We walked twenty minutes to buy groceries, an ordinary walk for most, but for me a reminder of my limits. That evening, she ordered food. Traveling required a discipline I was still learning to maintain.

On the wedding day, Kristianna wore a stunning yellow dress. She radiated a calm strength I could not name. I dressed to echo her color, yellow tie, matching pocket square, loafers. It was my way of saying, I am walking with you, even if slowly. I managed to find a suit in my closet that almost fit, close enough that I did not need to buy a new one, but the fabric still hung differently on my frame.

People were happy to see me. Warm smiles. Compliments. "You look great." "It's so good to see you." Their kindness touched me and unsettled me. Were they seeing me, or the memory of me?

I smiled, but inside, the conflict sharpened. This was the cruelty of recovery, mourning a self that only you know is gone, while the world continues to greet him as if he were intact.

I danced briefly. Less freely than before. I tired quickly. She offered to leave whenever I wanted. I nodded.

In the Uber back, I was silent. For most, the wedding would remain a beautiful memory. For me, it also became a symbol, the tension of participating in joy while carrying private grief.

That night, that balance was sustained by one person.

Kristianna.

SECTION XII — THE WAR WITH THE PEN

Some battles arrive quietly, disguised as minor inconveniences, yet carry the weight of an entire inner war.

For me, one such battle involved a pen and a blank page.

Before the stroke, writing was instinctive. My hand knew the way. My thoughts flowed into words with ease.

After the stroke, that familiar gesture became foreign.

My fingers hesitated.

The page transformed from freedom into battlefield, a place where the former self and the emerging self-confronted each other daily.

I began writing short scripts, one or two pages, in a notebook, rehearsed each morning to preserve a fragile connection between thought and hand.

Missing a day felt catastrophic, as though weeks of progress vanished overnight.

Thanksgiving intensified the struggle.

I wanted to send cards, as I always had. Each card took four times longer than before. My hand shook. Letters warped. A simple 8 became an ordeal.

Some days I signed my name dozens of times, hoping muscle memory would return.

A question haunted me.

How can a man with a doctorate struggle to write?

It was not an intellectual question.

It was an identity wound.

Writing is not merely a tool.

It is an extension of the self.

Losing it, even temporarily, exposed a vulnerability I had never known.

Yet beneath the humiliation, something refused to yield.

A stripped-down determination, detached from performance, rooted in survival.

Kristianna never missed an opportunity to tell me when my writing was beautiful. She said it only on days when the effort had been real.

Her words were not compliments.

They were anchors.

During those long sessions of trembling letters, another question emerged.

What does God restore first?

What does He restore last?

And what is He teaching us in between?

He did not return my hand all at once.

He did not immediately restore my voice or mental agility.

He restored patience first.

Looking back, I see that God often rebuilds the invisible before the visible.

Courage before competence.

Discipline before mastery.

Humility before form.

My shaky pages, broken numbers, uneven signatures were part of a silent liturgy.

Writing became more than a skill to recover.

It became a place of transformation.

I was not merely regaining the ability to write.

I was learning to inhabit each gesture with awareness.

To live with a trembling hand and a persevering heart.

CONCLUSION

This chapter has traced a particular kind of solitude, the solitude that emerges after the crisis, when the body begins to function again, but the interior world remains unsettled.

A solitude experienced amid visits, meals, travel, and celebration.

A solitude that exists even in love.

I could finally name it.

The distance between who I was and who I was becoming.

Between social image and interior truth.

Between the desire to be accompanied and the fear of becoming a burden.

As time passed, I sensed hesitation in others.

What should we say?

How should we say it?

Should we treat Radar as before, or as still fragile?

Their care did not change.

But a new tension appeared between us.

Not hostility.

Not rejection.

Uncertainty.

And I understood that I, too, was uncertain.

I did not yet know how to ask for what I needed. I did not know how to explain that visible improvement and inner restoration do not move at the same pace. I did not know how to help others approach me, because I was still learning how to approach myself.

That is why this solitude could not be solved simply by company.

It belonged to a deeper passage.

A passage through altered identity.

A passage through vulnerability.

A passage through the slow reconstruction of trust in one's own body, voice, mind, and place in the world.

What this chapter reveals is not the failure of love, but its limit.

Love can accompany.

Love can protect.

Love can feed, visit, drive, listen, wait, and remain.

But there comes a point in recovery when no one can cross the interior threshold for you.

No friend.

No spouse.

No family member.

No community.

There is a room within healing where the self must learn to stand again before God, before memory, before fear, before the mirror, before the future.

That room is lonely.

But it is not empty.

It is there that something new begins.

Not the old self restored exactly as before.

Not a triumphant return.

Something quieter.

Something more truthful.

A self-stripped of performance, forced into honesty, and slowly taught to live again from the inside out.

In that sense, solitude was not only my suffering.

It was also my teacher.

It exposed what support could not heal.

It revealed what progress could not measure.

It prepared the ground for a deeper work.

Because after the crisis, after the visits, after the milestones, after the effort to look normal again, another question remained.

How do you live when survival is no longer the only task?

That question opens the next stage of the journey.

6

WHEN OTHERS DON'T KNOW WHAT TO DO

When goodwill searches for a way

I remember a simple moment, almost banal: a hallway, a colleague, a handshake.

He said, "It's good to see you again."

I answered, "Thank you."

They saw my return. I was still arriving.

That was my first encounter with recovery in public.

My life had stopped. The world had not.

There is a season of recovery that belongs neither to the body nor to the soul. It belongs to other people.

It is not a season anyone prepares you for. No doctor tells you that the world around you may begin to hesitate. No therapist explains that healing will depend not only on medication, exercises, or rest, but also on that uncertain social space where other people search for the right way to stand beside you.

I discovered this season the way you discover a climate. You do not choose it, but it surrounds you.

It settles into details. A sentence placed awkwardly. A gaze that lingers too long. A silence that arrives without warning.

It is the season when those around you no longer know exactly who you have become, nor how to adjust to you.

In the earlier chapters, I followed the visible fractures: a rhythm broken, a body turned messenger, the inner storm, the paradox of healing, the solitude that follows illness. But another fracture remained. My illness had entered the eyes of others.

It did not fully belong to them, yet they carried some of its fragments.

Illness does not touch only the one who falls ill. It modifies the ecosystem around that person. It shifts relational landmarks. It rearranges roles. A diffuse tension appears, where everyone searches for the right posture without being sure what the right gesture might be.

This chapter lives in that fragile zone. Neither tragic nor heroic. Simply human.

It is the story of a season when people wanted to help but did not yet know how.

SECTION I — THE PUBLIC RETURN

When I came back to Asheville School, I genuinely believed my absence had left a visible void.

For me, everything had tipped. The trip. The hospital in Yaoundé. The stroke. The hesitant steps in the apartment. The CPAP. The weight loss. The broken voice.

But here, in this city where the mountains breathe calmly, the world had continued.

That contrast unsettled me more than I expected. I had imagined some trace of interruption, some evidence that what had happened to me had also altered the rhythm around me. Instead, the school hallways kept moving. Meetings had been held. Students had grown. Conversations had moved forward. Habits had re-formed around my absence.

People greeted me with relief.

"You're back. You look pretty good."

Something inside me tightened.

Not out of ingratitude, but out of mismatch.

I was physically present, emotionally behind, spiritually suspended.

They saw the return. I was still trying to inhabit it.

So I smiled so as not to embarrass anyone. I nodded so as not to worry anyone. I adjusted my tone so as not to disturb anyone.

During one of my first faculty meetings after returning, I chose a seat near the end of the room. The Head of School invited us into small group discussion, so we turned toward one another instead of toward a single speaker. I followed carefully, holding each thread in place so the conversation would not outrun me.

A colleague at my table asked for my perspective on a situation that once would have felt like natural terrain. The small circle shifted toward me. I began to answer and lost a word midway through the sentence. It did not disappear dramatically. It simply did not arrive. I paused longer than the moment required.

Someone gently supplied the word, and the discussion continued.

Nothing was wrong. No one reacted strongly. Yet inside I felt the distance between participation and presence. I was in the meeting, but I was also managing my place inside it, measuring breath, pacing thought, asking my voice to cooperate.

When the meeting ended, a few colleagues at my table thanked me for sharing and said it was good to have me back. I believed them. Still, I understood something new about community. Belonging is not only being welcomed into a room. Sometimes it is learning how to remain when the room moves faster than your current strength.

I walked out grateful and tired in a way that had less to do with work than with the quiet effort of being seen while still becoming.

That same truth met me in smaller moments too. A hallway. A colleague. A handshake.

"It's good to see you again."

"Thank you."

But inside another sentence rose quietly.

You see me again, yes. But you do not see me yet.

I was walking. I stood upright. I spoke. So to the world I was fine.

Inside, I was navigating between two versions of myself: the one I showed so that I could stand in the eyes of others, and the one I carried within me, fragile, tired, alert to every signal of the body, every tremor, every fog that might return.

I did not yet have language for it, but a relational gap had opened.

Others saw my return. They could not see the effort required to exist inside it.

SECTION II — WHEN OTHERS DON'T KNOW WHAT TO DO

There are phrases people said to me, meant to comfort me, that landed on my chest like a poorly placed stone.

"You're young, you'll recover fast."

I smiled. I was not sure.

"Thankfully, you can hardly see it."

I nodded. Nothing visible did not mean nothing real.

"You look great."

I had not slept the night before.

I understood the intention. It was kind. It simply missed me.

Love sometimes does not know where to place its hand.

Some people spoke loudly, as if I could not hear. Others softly, as if I might break. Advice arrived before questions. Encouragement came before stability. I often felt handled more than heard.

They were trying to get me back on my feet.

I was still learning where the ground was.

Some avoided the subject entirely. We spoke of schedules, weather, and ordinary updates. The absence of the subject filled the room more than the subject itself could have.

Others watched how I walked, how I held a glass, how long I spoke before pausing. Everyone was trying to meet me somewhere I could not yet stand.

Slowly I understood something simple. Illness does not break only a body. It unsettles the coherence around it. Relationships begin reorganizing before anyone knows how to name what has changed. Goodwill becomes awkward not because love is missing, but because the landmarks have shifted.

One Sunday at Trinity Presbyterian Church, just after the service, a man approached me. He smiled warmly, shook my hand, and asked where I was from. I answered slowly. The words came, but heavy, as if each one had to cross a small distance before reaching my mouth.

He listened without finishing my sentences or looking away. When I mentioned that I had suffered a stroke weeks earlier, his expression changed, but not in the way I had come to expect. He moved from surprise into steadiness. He did not rush into advice. He did not offer a quick reassurance to close the moment. He simply said he was glad I was there and hoped I would keep coming.

Nothing dramatic happened. We did not speak long. But as he walked away, I realized something had just occurred that was rarer than I knew how to name. The conversation required no performance. He met me at the pace I could offer.

For the first time in a public space, I was not trying to pass as recovered.

I was simply present.

SECTION III — THE NEW DISCOMFORT

Some people grew quiet around me.

Not from indifference. Often from fear.

Fear of saying the wrong thing. Fear of reminding me of the stroke. Fear of tiring me. Fear of entering a territory they did not know how to cross.

Sometimes the silence became its own language.

I am here, but I do not know how to be here.

Others moved in the opposite direction. Their attention intensified. Medical recommendations appeared. Comparisons surfaced with cousins, aunts, colleagues who had gone through something apparently similar.

I listened patiently, but inside I knew a stroke is never similar. It touches life exactly where it had once felt most stable.

Behind many conversations I sensed the same unspoken question:

Who are you now?

And how should I adjust to you?

I could not answer them.

Because I did not yet know myself.

That was part of the discomfort too. I was asking others for clarity I did not yet have. Illness had sharpened perception and blurred judgment. I interpreted hesitation too quickly. I read some silences as distance, some caution as rejection, some awkwardness as proof that I had become a burden.

Often the truth was simpler.

They did not know what to do because I did not yet know how to be received.

That realization softened something in me. Discomfort is rarely cruel. More often, it is love without a compass.

SECTION IV — THE CLOSE CIRCLE

The first person to live this confusion with me was Kristianna.

She carried my recovery, my food, my appointments, my fragility.

Nights were hardest. My body tried to sleep. My mind stayed on watch. I carried the memory of those moments when confusion had overtaken me and I had been rushed to the emergency room, unsure of what my own mind was doing. I feared slipping back into that state. I feared waking disoriented. I feared not waking at all.

The possibility of another stroke remained in the background of my nights like a low sound that never completely stopped.

Even when my body tried to rest, my thoughts stayed alert, scanning for signs, replaying symptoms, guarding against shadows that became bolder after dark.

The night brought quiet, but not peace.

Kristianna carried that reality with me.

She also had to navigate the outside world. She had to decide what needed to be said and what could be allowed to pass. She had to judge when to protect me, when to encourage me, when to step in, when to let me struggle.

I often saw her hesitate.

Should she let me walk alone?

Should she correct me in public?

Should she supply a forgotten word?

Should she explain a face I could no longer read?

I was learning dependence.

She was learning vigilance.

No one prepares a spouse for that role. It is a vocation born from emergency, a ministry improvised in hospital rooms, living rooms, and ordinary days that no longer feel ordinary.

There is a fatigue spouses carry quietly. The fatigue of monitoring breathing. The fatigue of measuring energy. The fatigue of keeping the world stable while the other person learns again how to stand.

Friends lived another version of the same tension.

I saw generosity in their eyes and caution in their gestures. With some, warmth returned naturally. Laughter rose. Cameroon entered the room again. For a moment I felt almost intact.

With others, hesitation appeared. They looked for the man from before. Not finding him in quite the same way, they searched. Questions came too precise or not precise enough. Congratulations arrived when I felt broken. Sports talk moved across the table while my body trembled slightly beneath it.

They saw a visit.

I felt a performance.

One late afternoon, a friend asked me to meet him near a coffee shop downtown. We chose a table outside. People passed with ordinary purpose. The hour required nothing from me except presence.

He asked how I was doing, not politely but patiently.

I began to answer and stopped midway through the sentence, checking whether my voice would remain clear. He did not interrupt. He waited.

After a moment he said quietly that he was not in a hurry.

No advice followed. Just permission.

We spoke of ordinary things again. Work. Weather. A book he was reading. Ease returned slowly, not because my body had changed, but because I no longer had to perform steadiness.

For the first time in public, I was not appearing recovered.

I was being accompanied.

SECTION V — SOCIAL REPOSITIONING

At school, the dynamic became more complex.

Some colleagues wanted to protect me, to spare me, to give me all the time I needed. Others assumed I had returned as I was before and expected the same pace, the same energy, the same availability.

I tried not to blame anyone. They saw my silhouette in meetings, my steady walk down the hallway, my presence in familiar spaces. From the outside the conclusion seemed obvious.

He has recovered.

Inside, I was still moving through a dense fog. I tracked words that threatened to disappear before arriving. I felt fatigue rise like a wave. I calculated how many sentences I could still manage. Behind apparent normalcy stood a monumental effort.

Then something subtler appeared.

Not hostility.

Repositioning.

A greeting missing. A conversation closing when I arrived. A reply delayed just long enough to speak. A room that once opened easily now requiring some new proof of self.

My presence was being renegotiated.

Illness does not only wound a body. It disorganizes relationships. Everyone must learn a new way to meet what seems, from a distance, like the same person.

This was especially difficult because I often misread care as distance and hesitation as rejection. Illness had made me more perceptive and less certain at the same time. I sometimes asked others for the clarity I did not yet possess within myself.

Still, not everything I sensed was imagined. Vulnerability has a way of exposing what performance once concealed. When old energy weakens, the gaze of others sometimes reveals what it truly believed.

Relationships reorganized. Some deepened, some loosened, some paused as if waiting for a version of me I could not yet confirm.

SECTION VI — RELATIONAL HEALING

I began to notice fatigue around me that was not mine.

Some came closer. Others grew quiet. Not from lack of love, but from not knowing where to stand.

I was not the only one exhausted. My illness carried with it a whole constellation of fatigues: the fatigue of those who love you, the fatigue of those who fear another episode, the emotional fatigue of adjusting to your fluctuations, the mental fatigue of guessing what you need, the quiet fatigue of seeing you fragile when they had always known you as strong.

That fatigue is rarely named.

Yet it shapes relationships. It creates distance between what people feel and what they dare to say. Some remain present but uncertain. Others slowly pull away. Not always from indifference. Sometimes from lack of bearings.

That too became part of what I had to understand. Illness does not stay inside one body. The wound spreads into the relationship around it.

Healing begins when people learn how to stand near each other again.

There were moments of silent grace that taught me this more convincingly than any explanation could. Someone sitting with me a few minutes and saying very little. A meal left at the door. A prayer sent by voice message. A hand on the shoulder without commentary. Eyes that said enough.

You are still here.

And I am here too.

I was not healing alone. Through those gestures, ordinary and almost hidden, God was quietly repairing something in me.

Slowly I stopped assuming intention too quickly. I began to understand that others were also losing the version of me they knew how to love. They were learning me again while I was learning myself again.

My healing was happening in them too.

CONCLUSION

What this season finally taught me is that healing is not decided only by what the body recovers.

It is also decided by what the soul no longer has to carry alone.

At first, the tension seemed to live outside me. It appeared in the awkwardness of others, in their silences, their hesitations, and their sincere but poorly placed gestures. I thought the question was how they would position themselves in the face of my fragility.

Gradually I understood that something deeper was taking place.

While others searched for the right way to stand around me, I was losing my place within myself.

I could walk. I could speak. I could work.

But I no longer knew where I stood.

The world around me no longer knew how to help me.

And I no longer knew how to belong.

That is where the conflict changed level. It no longer concerned only others. It passed through me.

And it is precisely there, where identity begins to waver and belonging is no longer self-evident, that the next chapter begins.

7

BELONGING AFTER ILLNESS

When Identity Wavers, Belonging Fractures

Before the stroke, presence did not require attention. I entered conversations without measuring how much of me I could afford to spend. Words came, and the body supported the moment without asking for permission. I did not think about continuity because it held on its own.

After the stroke, presence became something I had to manage. I could still enter a room, still greet, still answer. But every interaction required a quiet calculation.

How long could I stay attentive?

How carefully did I need to speak?

Should I finish the sentence, or preserve the energy to remain steady a few minutes longer?

I counted energy.

Nothing dramatic announced the change. There was no clear line separating before and after. Belonging rarely disappears all at once. It recedes when the self you bring into a space no longer moves at the same speed as the one others expect.

It is there, in that almost nothing, that silence begins to settle.

SECTION I — IDENTITY AND FRACTURE

After the stroke, I could still enter spaces. I could still smile. I could still greet. I could still show up.

But showing up is not the same as arriving.

I would step into a conversation and feel immediately that I was late to myself, as if the man people were addressing and the man inside my chest had not fully synchronized yet.

A name would not come back. A thought would evaporate in the middle of a sentence. A wave of fatigue would rise during an interaction and turn attention into labor.

I was speaking. I was working, partially and cautiously. So from the outside, it made sense to assume I was fine.

But inwardly, I was living something else. I was carrying the effort of remaining legible while I was still learning the contours of my own change.

SECTION II — RETURNING TO WORK

When I returned to Asheville School, I discovered that it was possible to be both at home and a stranger in the same space.

From October to December, my physician authorized me to work two days a week. Then, from January to early March, that rhythm continued, two days, usually Monday or Tuesday, and then Thursday. After spring break, I was allowed to move to three days a week until the end of the school year. I learned quickly that the hardest part was not showing up. It was recovering from showing up.

On the days I was on campus, the school continued to operate at full speed. Students moved quickly from one building to another. Teachers flowed from classes to meetings to athletic practices. Emails had not waited for my brain to reorganize itself. Projects, tensions, and initiatives all continued. I arrived with a body still in recovery, a mind forced to conserve every drop of concentration, and a voice that sometimes had to choose between speaking now or preserving itself long enough to make it through the rest of the day. The gap between the institution's pace and my temporary capacities created a constant silent tension.

I remember my first days clearly. I walked into my office and felt as though I were visiting someone else's space. I opened my computer and felt that strange mixture of familiarity and distance. I came across files, emails, and meeting notes from before the stroke, like carefully archived remains of another version of myself.

My hand paused on the door handle for a second longer than it used to, as if my body needed permission to enter my own life.

In the hallways, many faces were warm. Most of my colleagues cared deeply about my wellbeing. Some wrote to me. Others welcomed me back with genuine words.

"We're glad to see you."

"Take your time."

"Your health comes first."

The Head of School said to me one day, "Your main job right now is to stay healthy."

And then there was the other reality, quieter and more painful.

Some people changed their attitude toward me, and not for the better. They were colleagues, people with whom I had made real efforts to build and maintain good working relationships. Before the stroke, I had stretched myself for them. I had occupied mediation spaces that were not mine to hold. I had absorbed tensions that did not belong to me, often quietly and often without recognition.

After the stroke, something shifted.

I do not know exactly why. People responded differently, and my new limits exposed what I had been carrying for years.

What I do know is this: my capacity to get out of my own way for the sake of others had changed. Social interactions required more energy. Speaking demanded more effort. The social anxiety that accompanied recovery made certain exchanges feel heavier, slower, more exposed. I could no longer compensate for discomfort by being endlessly agreeable or perpetually available.

There were also individuals whose posture toward me confirmed what I had sensed before but had chosen not to name fully. I had already noticed patterns of dismissiveness, subtle self-interest, or a lack of reciprocity. Before the stroke, I had given those dynamics the benefit of the doubt. I told myself that complexity deserved patience, that people were more than their worst moments. I stayed generous, hoping it would change something.

I was trying to take the high road, not performatively, but deliberately. I wanted to model a lesson I believed in deeply, that dignity does not require retaliation, that integrity is not contingent on how others behave, and that it is possible to remain principled without becoming hardened.

The stroke complicated that aspiration, not because it made me smaller, but because it stripped away my ability to sustain relationships that relied on my self-erasure. What once looked like generosity began to reveal itself as imbalance. What once felt like patience began to feel like self-betrayal.

The change in how some colleagues related to me was painful, but it was also clarifying. It forced me to confront a difficult realization: not every relationship I had been working to preserve was meant to survive the version of me that emerged after the stroke.

Those lessons settled not only in my thinking, but in my body. Once they settled there, they could no longer be ignored.

SECTION III — INVISIBLE WOUNDS

I cannot say that the school, as an institution, rejected me. That would be unfair.

But I can say that certain individual behaviors left marks.

There were a few people who, rather than reaching out, seemed to distance themselves further. I cannot know what was happening in them. I only know how it landed in me. I began to feel optional.

I said good morning.

The face in front of me passed through me as if I were air.

My voice sounded louder to me than it should have.

When you are already down, even a small gesture of contempt feels like a kick.

I kept walking as if nothing had happened, but my pace changed without my permission.

A withheld greeting can feel like a sentence. You matter less than you used to.

These moments did not remain where they occurred. They lodged elsewhere, in the gaps of my days, in the way I stepped into my office in the morning, in my hesitation to speak during meetings, in the moral fatigue that followed an interaction that appeared, on the surface, ordinary.

Nothing dramatic happened, yet the body kept the score.

I replayed the hallway for the rest of the morning without deciding to.

Fighting to belong in spaces where some people refuse even to say hello to you, while you are in recovery, is not generosity. It is programmed exhaustion.

SECTION IV — RECLAIMING PLACE

Toward the end of that first school year after the stroke, something shifted inside me.

I realized that continuing to seek validation from those who had no real interest in seeing me as a human being with limits and needs was only prolonging my suffering. It meant maintaining a constant, unnecessary, exhausting inner conflict.

So I made a simple but radical decision.

I remember standing in the hallway after a brief exchange and not turning back to repair it. My chest tightened, waited for the familiar pull to return, and then slowly settled.

I would no longer let my inner steadiness depend on the gaze of people who had no intention of meeting me with basic dignity. I would no longer allow my value to be negotiated in the eyes of those who had no intention of recognizing it.

I am an immigrant who worked hard to earn a doctorate. I came from another continent, another system, with a family, cultural, and spiritual history that does not always fit neatly into existing frameworks. I lived through an illness that could have left me with severe and lasting impairments.

And despite all of that, I am here.

I could feel my feet more firmly on the floor as I thought it.

So I began to shift my gaze. Less toward those who closed doors. More toward those who left them open. Less toward those who avoided a simple greeting. More toward those who checked in, even awkwardly.

I began leaving conversations when they ended, not when they softened.

Reclaiming my belonging was not about fighting a battle. It was about ending a quiet war against myself.

And without naming it right away, my body began to respond to that shift. When I stopped fighting to be tolerated, my nervous system stopped living as though it were constantly under threat.

I noticed that I no longer rehearsed the day on my way home.

It was not peace yet.

But it was no longer struggle.

I sat in my office one afternoon and realized I was not bracing for the next interaction.

And in that space, calmer, truer, and more stripped down, something in me began to return.

SECTION V — RACE AND PERSPECTIVE

Working within an institution where people of different origins, ages, identities, and belief systems coexist inevitably means navigating multiple perspectives.

When you are a Black person in a predominantly white environment, you do not arrive alone. You enter carrying centuries of history, even when no one names it.

When you are an immigrant, you carry different ways of understanding authority, community, respect, and dignity.

When you have survived a stroke, you add another layer, one marked by acknowledged fragility, temporary dependence, and a body that now enforces its own limits.

I began to notice it in ordinary exchanges. A greeting that used to be easy became thin. A question was answered with less patience. A face tightened when I did not move fast enough. In those moments, it was not disagreement. It was a quiet demotion.

And if there was one place where this tension became visible without anyone raising their voice, it was Civil Rights Day.

SECTION VI — CIVIL RIGHTS DAY

Civil Rights Day at Asheville School is a day when we pause the regular academic schedule so our community can reflect on how we treat one another and who we are becoming together. We hold it on the day that honors Martin Luther King Jr., not only to remember him, but to remember his conviction that a society is judged by how it protects the dignity of the most vulnerable, and that love must show itself in action. The day is less about studying the past and more about paying attention in the present, where listening, discomfort, and honesty become part of learning how to live with dignity alongside others.

In previous years, Civil Rights Day had been followed by feedback, conversations, and sometimes openly expressed disagreement. That year, there was nothing. No conversation. No questions. No engagement. Only silence from colleagues.

What I did not expect was how deeply it affected me.

It was my second Civil Rights Day in this role. I was still in recovery. I learned about criticism only through indirect echoes, comments relayed secondhand, fragments without context or conversation. No one came to speak to me directly. No one asked about my intentions. No one questioned my interpretation in my presence. No one opened a space for dialogue.

During recovery, unresolved tension never remains abstract. When it is neither addressed nor shared, it does not disappear. It settles. It becomes an additional burden, unseen, unspoken, but very real. My body, already sensitive, registered that weight immediately.

What stayed with me most, though, was not only what I did not hear from adults. It was what I heard from students.

A few of them came up to me afterward, quietly and without ceremony, and thanked me. Some were direct. Others were almost hesitant, as if unsure whether they were supposed to say anything at all. But they did. They looked me in the eye and said something simple, that the day mattered to them, that they felt seen, that something in the program made them think, or made them feel proud, or made them feel less alone.

I did not interpret this as a simple story of good and bad people. Silence comes from many places, fear of saying the wrong thing, exhaustion, private disagreement, uncertainty, or the belief that disengagement is safer than honesty.

Silence never erases tension. It only relocates it.

JANUARY 21, 2025 — WHEN BELONGING BECOMES SHARED WORK

January 21, 2025, was a radically different experience.

That year's theme was Civil Rights and Activism, and from the beginning, the vision was clear: students would be at the center, not symbolically, but concretely. They were not invited simply to participate. They were entrusted to lead. They facilitated. They spoke. They danced. They sang. They conducted interviews. They led quizzes. They projected short video clips. They delivered speeches grounded not only in historical research, but also in lived experience.

What unfolded that day was not a program designed to be consumed, but a collective effort that required preparation, vulnerability, and shared responsibility.

The Black Student Union played a central role, carrying the day with remarkable composure, courage, and joy. Their leadership was not ornamental. It was grounded, thoughtful, and steady. They held the space with a seriousness that never extinguished their lightness, and with a confidence that did not need permission to exist.

Teachers from multiple departments devoted hours, often unseen, to rehearsals and preparation. Together with students, they worked through musical performances, choreographed dance pieces, refined speeches, and shaped poems that spoke directly to the themes of the day. Nothing was improvised casually. Every element required intention, trust, and care. Music carried memory. Movement held history in the body. Words, spoken and written, asked for attention rather than comfort.

Students and faculty facilitated workshops side by side, not as experts delivering content, but as co-learners willing to sit with complexity and listen across difference. Hierarchy softened. Collaboration became visible. The work itself modeled what it was trying to teach.

I was intentionally attentive to involving as many academic disciplines as possible, not for optics, but for meaning. When multiple departments engage, a message is sent that cannot be reduced to a slogan: belonging is not owned by a single office, an identity group, or one day on the calendar. It is collective work. It lives in shared labor, shared risk, and shared accountability.

When belonging is isolated, it becomes fragile. When it is shared, it becomes durable. It moves from performance to practice.

As the day unfolded, my body registered something unfamiliar. Not adrenaline. Not vigilance. But lightness. Space. A sense that the weight was not resting solely on me. The work was being held by students, by colleagues, and by the structure itself. For the first time in a long while, I was not absorbing tension alone. I was witnessing it being distributed and carried together.

My body understood before I did. When the weight was shared, I stopped bracing. That day, my body felt the difference before my mind fully named it.

It did not mean everything was resolved. It did not mean everyone was comfortable. But it meant something essential had shifted. Belonging was no longer being asked of me alone. It was being practiced by the community.

And that distinction, subtle, embodied, and unmistakable, stayed with me long after the day ended.

DR. CARTER — CATALYSTS AND COMPANIONSHIP

The keynote speaker that day was Dr. Carter. I have known him since the fall of 2016, when I began my doctoral program. We took several courses together. He later invited me as a keynote speaker at his conference for three consecutive years. I worked for him. We traveled together. He completed his doctorate a few years before I did, but he never left me alone.

After the stroke, on October 6, he came to visit me. I was still deeply affected, physically and emotionally, but his presence mattered more than words.

That day, he approached the life of Martin Luther King Jr. through the notion of the catalyst, those formative moments, influences, and ruptures that shape commitment.

"People Must Really Love You"

Dr. Carter stayed until the end of the program. He observed student performances. He watched faculty engagement. He noticed the co-ordination, the trust, the collective investment.

At one point, he turned to me and said something simple, but decisive:

"People at your workplace must really love you to do all of this for you. You are blessed."

Since the stroke, few words have resonated as deeply.

Because what he named was not popularity.

It was belonging.

Not because I was impressive, but because I could recognize myself again inside shared work.

Not the kind that comes from approval, but the kind revealed through shared labor, mutual trust, and chosen presence.

In that precise moment, something in me settled. For the first time since the illness, I did not merely feel tolerated or professionally accepted.

I felt carried.

And my body recognized the difference.

Civil Rights Day became more than a commemoration. It became a living practice, a collective act of repair. And for me, it became proof that belonging, when shared, can carry even a body in reconstruction.

SECTION VII — AGENCY AND INTERDEPENDENCE

A colleague I deeply respect has invited me into her ninth-grade life skills classes to lead two workshops.

The first workshop centers on belonging, personal agency, and responsibility. We invite students to reflect on moments when they felt included and moments when they did not, and to consider how their own choices and behaviors shape those experiences.

The second workshop moves into more delicate territory, finding belonging through conflict resolution in high school. I was working with a group of freshmen, students between thirteen and fifteen years old, at a private school where small class sizes allow for sustained attention and real relationship building.

We explored the hopes and fears they carried before arriving on campus, many of them leaving home for the first time, and how unresolved internal tensions can quietly erode a sense of place. In a setting where expectations are high and visibility is constant, students learn quickly how to perform competence. What they struggle to name is how much energy it takes to keep parts of themselves hidden in order to belong.

The conversation was not abstract. It was grounded in their daily lives, friendships that felt fragile, academic pressure that never fully quieted, moments of isolation that came without warning. What emerged was not resistance, but relief. Relief at being invited to speak honestly about the inner negotiations they had already begun to make.

In that room, I saw the pattern in its simplest form. What they carried quietly was already shaping their place in the group.

Before the stroke, these sessions fit naturally into my professional rhythm. I arrived prepared. I delivered the content. I facilitated discussion. I left with the sense that students had received words and tools that mattered.

After the stroke, the workshops did not change.

I did.

During the session on belonging, I now choose deliberately to place myself at the center of the conversation, not as an expert, but as an example.

I tell students the truth.

Before the stroke, my posture itself communicated confidence. I believed, perhaps too easily, that belonging depended primarily on me. That it was my responsibility to include others, read the room, create space, and regulate the emotional climate. I understood belonging as agency exercised outward.

The stroke dismantled that narrative.

My confidence was visibly affected. Crowds became intimidating. I no longer entered spaces with the same physical presence. My pace slowed. My voice softened. I became quieter, more cautious.

And for the first time in my adult life, I experienced belonging not as something I produced, but as something I needed.

I tell students that I could have withdrawn. I could have turned inward and allowed vulnerability to harden into isolation. Instead, slowly and imperfectly, I learned that I needed others. Not their pity. Their intention.

I needed people to include me patiently in conversations so I could remain myself in the room. I needed others to pause and ask what I thought. I needed inclusion practiced not as charity, but as shared responsibility.

Saying this out loud, naming that need publicly, was unexpectedly healing. The strain no longer had to be carried alone. My body no longer had to arbitrate it in silence.

It forced me to confront an internal tension I had carried for years without naming it, independence and interdependence. Strength and need.

The stroke did not create that tension.

It revealed it.

In the second workshop, focused on finding belonging through conflict resolution, vulnerability deepened further.

I tell students that the stroke confronted me with a challenge I had never anticipated: I could no longer speak freely. Even today, speech is something I approach consciously. I must open my mouth deliberately, articulate each syllable with care, remain attentive to the heaviness that can suddenly settle into my tongue.

This challenge awakened a fear I had never associated with myself, the fear of public speaking. Ironically, the space where I once felt most alive became charged with risk.

I name the internal tension simply and clearly: fear of failure and the need to take risks. The desire to withdraw and the call to move forward.

And what I want students to understand, and what I myself had to learn, is this: when internal struggle remains unspoken, it isolates. But when it is named, shared appropriately and intentionally, it can become a point of connection.

Opening myself publicly about my internal struggles did not diminish my belonging.

It restored it.

Today, when I stand in those classrooms, I am no longer simply facilitating lessons.

I am embodying them.

I am showing what it means to remain in a community while changing.

Still, there was one place where belonging had once felt effortless to me, a place where I never had to translate myself, and that was the court.

SECTION VIII — BASKETBALL AND DISPLACEMENT

For a very long time, basketball was more than a sport for me. It was a language. A territory. A place where I knew exactly who I was and what I was worth.

I was first a player. I wore the jersey of the Cameroonian national team. In the United States, I played on a Division I scholarship.

Then I became a coach.

Very early on, I knew one thing with almost instinctive clarity: I did not want to be someone's assistant. This was not arrogance, nor a refusal to collaborate. It ran deeper. I understood that the way a team functions, the distribution of responsibilities, the quality of relationships, the attention given to secondary voices, depends first and foremost on leadership.

Being a head coach meant being able to create a framework where people did not merely fit in, but could truly belong.

At New Hampton School, where I coached the Varsity B team in the MOSAIC league, we won two consecutive championships. But what I am most proud of does not appear in any statistic: I always made sure my assistants felt included, considered, and invested. I trusted them. I wanted them fully in.

Later, at Monarch High School, I chose to be the head coach of the junior varsity team rather than an assistant with varsity. It was not about prestige. It was about internal coherence.

So before the stroke, when the former head coach of the varsity basketball team at Asheville School contacted me to become his assistant, on top of my academic role, I hesitated for a long time.

I had never sought out an assistant coaching role. For years, I had been clear about that. I value responsibility, voice, and shared authority, and I knew myself well enough to know that I would struggle in a position defined primarily by execution without participation. So when the opportunity first came up, I hesitated.

What made this situation different was not the title. It was the relationship.

The conversations were honest from the beginning. I was told clearly that I would be included, not as an extra set of hands, but as a full partner in the work. Practice planning. Game strategy. Player development. The daily decisions that shape a team's culture. There was no promise of hierarchy dissolving, but there was a commitment to collaboration.

That mattered to me.

I agreed because trust was present, the kind that shows itself in how people listen, how they share responsibility, and how they make room for one another's expertise. We developed mutual respect, and with it, mutual confidence. I believed that my voice would be heard, that my experience would be valued, and that the work would be shared rather than managed.

The first two years confirmed that belief. There was real professional chemistry. Complementarity. A rhythm that allowed each of us to lead without competing. I felt useful. I felt included. I felt, in a very concrete way, in my place.

When he accepted a Division I coaching position, I participated in recruiting his replacement. During that transition, I served as interim head coach and led spring practices.

Then, during the summer, I had a stroke. Once again, the body spoke before words could follow.

The new coach and his family brought us a meal. Human gesture. Sincere. I did not participate in fall practices. When I returned, just before the season, I could be present, but not as before. Speaking required immense effort. I tired quickly. I took breaks during practice. I did not travel for away games. I tried to be a good teammate.

At the end of the season, I proposed a precise plan to improve our defense. He entrusted me with spring practices. Returning to the court, guiding, transmitting, restored some confidence.

The following summer, I worked at his Nike camp. It was fluid. Almost reparative.

The next season, I requested a clear meeting. I needed to know where I stood. We agreed that I would participate in practice planning, video analysis, and strategy. It made sense.

Then Hurricane Helene reached Western North Carolina. I want to name this carefully. It was not a simple flood in Asheville. Whole communities were overturned. Some lost homes. Some lost work. Some lost people they loved. A national emergency response was required, and life did not return to normal when the water receded. Recovery is still ongoing.

The campus closed. Without water, electricity, and cellphone service, we had to leave.

My wife and I, like most employees at the school, live in an on-campus apartment provided by the institution. When the utilities failed, staying was no longer possible.

He opened his home to us.

Those days mattered more than I understood at the time. Removed from schedules, practices, and institutional roles, what remained was something quieter and more durable. We shared meals. We waited together. We talked without urgency. We sat in the same uncertainty, not as colleagues navigating a crisis, but as people making room for one another.

Not the kind of closeness built on convenience or professional alignment, but the kind formed when vulnerability is shared without calculation. In those days, trust moved out of theory and into practice. Long before any shift became visible on the surface, something had already been set in place beneath it.

But when the season resumed, something shifted.

I discovered practice plans five minutes before sessions. I was not involved in video. I did not lead any drills. My voice faded slowly.

One evening, Kristianna came to watch a game. Later, she told me she had never had such a hard time watching me sit on a bench, not because the team was losing, but because I was no longer there. Not really.

She asked me if I still wanted to coach.

That question passed through me like a shockwave.

What I was experiencing was not only professional disappointment. It was a deep internal struggle. Each day, I felt a dull tension rise inside me, the need to prove my worth and fight for visibility while trying to protect my health.

That tension was not abstract. It registered in my fatigue. In my recovery. In my stability.

The more invisible I felt, the more I tried to compensate. And the more I compensated, the further I moved from healing.

I confided in a close friend, the head coach of the football team, Coach Shawn Bryson. He is a big man with a gentle presence, soft spoken and steady. What stayed with me was the calm he carried into responsibility.

We agreed that I should finish the season for the sake of the players. Then he asked me a simple question.

"Would you be interested in football next year?"

Without hesitation, I said yes.

A junior varsity basketball game, on a day when the assistant coach could not be there, became a turning point for me. I was given my voice back. I was asked what I saw. I spoke during timeouts and in the locker room.

The junior varsity basketball coach, Dave Coltrain, carried himself with a quiet integrity. Being around him felt clear and safe.

I felt something come back to life in me. I could breathe again. I was present.

After the game, I asked if he would accept me as an assistant. He said yes immediately.

That was belonging.

I had a courageous conversation with the varsity basketball coach. I spoke in facts. In expectations. In respect. In what was good for my health. Without accusation. Without collapse.

The change was approved.

And if work and sport showed me how belonging can be granted or withdrawn, home showed me something harder, because at home you cannot perform belonging. You have to live it.

SECTION IX — FAMILY BELONGING

If work exposed one form of displacement, family revealed another, quieter, more intimate, and often more difficult to name.

Illness does not only alter the one who falls.

It reorganizes the entire relational system around that fall.

At home, I was no longer the same man who had left for Cameroon. And yet everyone around me was still learning how to relate to me as if I were.

Kristianna carried more than anyone else.

She carried my recovery schedules, my moments of confusion, and the fears that rose at night without warning.

But she also carried something less visible: the responsibility of helping me belong to myself again without ever making me feel diminished.

That balance is almost impossible.

Too much help can feel like erasure.

Too little can feel like abandonment.

She had to decide, moment by moment, whether to intervene or step back, to correct a word or let it go, to protect me or let me struggle. And there was no guide, no protocol, no certainty.

I watched her learn in real time. I watched her hesitate before answering questions for me in public. I watched her scan my face to see if I was tiring. I watched her absorb my frustration when I could not express myself clearly. And I also watched her carry her own fatigue quietly.

I did not always know how to thank her. Sometimes I did not even know how to see what she was carrying.

Illness altered our dynamic. Not our love, but our rhythm.

I was slower. More cautious. More inward.

She was more alert. More anticipatory. More burdened.

Belonging within marriage is often assumed. But after illness, it must be renegotiated, not because commitment disappears, but because roles shift.

I was no longer only a husband. I was also a patient.

And she was no longer only my partner. She was also my anchor.

This created a silent tension, one that neither of us named early on.

How do you remain equals when one depends on the other for stability?

How do you protect dignity while offering care?

How do you love without overextension?

That tension did not erupt. It lingered. It showed itself in small frictions, in fatigue, in unspoken expectations.

But over time, something else emerged.

We began to speak more carefully. More honestly. More slowly.

I learned to say when I was overwhelmed.

She learned to step back when I needed space.

Belonging within our marriage became less about roles and more about presence. Not what I could provide. Not what she could manage. But how we could remain together inside uncertainty.

It required something rare: patience with a version of the person you love that neither of you fully understands yet.

CONCLUSION — SILENCE AND THRESHOLD

As the months passed, one truth became unavoidable.

The most difficult part of recovery was not physical weakness.

It was not cognitive slowness.

It was not even fear.

It was silence.

Not the silence of rest, nor the silence that invites truth, but the silence of misunderstanding.

After the initial concern faded, after the messages slowed, after the visits became less frequent, I entered a quieter phase, one where people assumed I was better and therefore no longer needed the same attentiveness.

I was walking.

I was working.

I was present.

But internally, I was still negotiating every movement, every sentence, every expectation.

I began to notice how rarely people asked how I was beyond surface politeness.

"How are you doing?" had become a greeting, not an inquiry.

I answered automatically.

"I'm doing well."

The words sat in my throat like something unfinished.

Not because they were fully true, but because it was easier than explaining a reality that had no shared vocabulary.

And so people retreat, not out of cruelty, but out of uncertainty.

In that silence, I began to listen differently.

For the first time, I was no longer rushing to fill space.

I was no longer performing competence.

I was no longer proving resilience.

I was simply present with what remained.

It was a quieter self.

A more attentive self.

A self no longer defined by output, speed, or endurance.

Who am I when I stop striving to be understood?

Can belonging survive without explanation?

I did not need answers yet.

I needed to stay.

I needed to listen.

I needed to learn how to live without performing my way back into safety.

It demanded presence.

And presence was enough to end Part II.

Not because the war was finished, but because I was finished running from what it was teaching me.

Not endurance.

Integration.

PART III

BECOMING WHOLE AGAIN

8

TRUTHS THAT RISE IN THE SILENCE

When belonging stabilizes and the inside begins to speak

The house is quiet longer than it used to be.

Morning light reaches the table and stays there.

No message asks for an answer. No schedule pushes the hour forward.

My body waits for urgency the way it once waited for breath after running.

Nothing comes.

I sit with coffee cooling beside my hand and realize I do not know what to do with time that is not demanded.

For years peace meant pressure I could manage.

This feels different.

The first part of my story was about movement.

The second was about survival.

What followed required something else.

Not resignation. Consent.

Consenting to the life that remained instead of chasing the life that collapsed.

One morning I woke up without pain and without urgency.

No appointment. No exercise to catch up on. No proof to produce.

I sat at the edge of the bed longer than necessary because nothing was asking me to hurry.

My body waited for instruction.

None came.

The day did not demand recovery. It simply began.

Chapter 7 ended where I stopped fighting to belong.

Not because everything was solved, but because something decisive had finally been understood. Fighting to be recognized in spaces that refuse to truly see you costs too much. And my body no longer agreed to pay that price.

I remember that shift with precision. The major emergencies had passed. The tests slowed. Medical appointments thinned out. I was no longer rushing through hospital corridors.

And the world restarted without asking me.

In Asheville School, I felt it as a quiet violence.

Students laughed in the hallways. Meetings recovered their rhythm. Calendars filled again.

People passed me, greeted me, asked, often with real sincerity,

How are you?

Are you better?

I said yes. I meant it, at least partly. But that yes no longer carried the same weight. Because after the storm, what remains is not peace.

What remains is silence.

Not the silence I choose. The silence that forces me to stay.

I came to see that the body does not invent anything. It reveals.

Illness did not punish. It broke the rhythm.

So this silence was not an ending. It was a threshold.

And the first truth that imposed itself was the most uncomfortable. It did not concern the stroke as an event. It concerned what I had been calling normal long before the stroke arrived.

SECTION I — THE TRUTH ABOUT HOW I WAS LIVING

Before the stroke, my pace felt normal because everyone was moving that fast.

That is how danger becomes ordinary.

In environments where people carry responsibility, education, leadership, care, faith, accompaniment, excess can disguise itself as virtue. Long days become proof of loyalty. Permanent availability becomes a sign of commitment. Fatigue becomes background noise you learn to ignore.

I had gotten used to it.

I remember a morning not long after returning to Asheville. It was still dark. The house was quiet. I got up early, by reflex more than decision. I stood in the kitchen without turning on the overhead light. I listened to the hum of the refrigerator, the soft silence of a sleeping home, and I looked at the clock.

My first thought was not fear. Not panic.

It was simply this.

I can still hold.

I stood there long enough for the coffee to grow cold.

That sentence did not surprise me. It felt intimate. I had been saying it inside for years.

Holding had become an identity posture.

Holding the roles.

Holding expectations.

Holding other people.

Holding the rhythm.

And I did it well. Too well.

Director.

Teacher.

Coach.

Mediator.

Husband.

Son.

Friend.

Man of faith.

I moved from one identity to the next without letting any of them be incomplete. Not out of vanity. Out of fidelity, or at least that is what I told myself.

If you had asked me back then what my mission was, I would have answered quickly.

To build.

To heal.

To help people feel good about themselves.

People had told me more than once that I was a healer, that they entered my life and left feeling lighter, steadier, somehow restored. I did not know how to measure the truth of that claim, but I recognized its contours.

I believed my mission was to build spaces that could hold people.

I wanted those who crossed my path to leave feeling seen.

It was true.

It was not complete.

What about what I wanted?

What about what I needed?

Beneath my generosity lived a deep inclination to please, to go beyond what was asked, to secure belonging through excess availability.

Before the stroke, this pattern felt like love.

After the stroke, it revealed itself as something else.

A quiet self-erasure dressed as service.

The signals had always been there.

Persistent fatigue. Light sleep. Short breath. Low, constant tension.

Nothing that looked like an emergency.

Everything that was, in my body.

I did not call it imbalance. I called it discipline.

Rest became something I earned, never something I honored. Slowness felt irresponsible. Stillness felt suspicious. I told myself I was built for intensity, that this was the normal price of a meaningful life.

Beneath it was belonging anxiety.

If I slow down, do I still matter?

If I say no, do I disappoint?

If I stop, do I lose my place?

I did not always think those questions.

I carried them.

The illness did not create this truth. It interrupted the narrative that kept me from seeing it.

After the stroke, I could no longer resolve every tension through performance. I could not convert every discomfort into productivity. The body stopped cooperating with that logic.

And in that confrontation, I had to recognize something difficult.

My value was intact.

My identity was not.

I believed in grace. I prayed. I trusted God. And yet, without saying it, I had absorbed a silent clause.

Holding on was faithfulness.

Stopping was failure.

In the silence, an old sentence from Scripture arrived as invitation.

Be still and know that I am God.

That was the instruction.

I was not living badly.

I was living above myself for too long.

And my body refused to live there with me anymore.

Once that truth was seen, it could no longer be ignored.

SECTION II — THE TRUTH ABOUT LIMITS

Limits were no longer a concept.

Limits became the rules of my days.

Before the stroke, I believed I knew my limits. In truth, I mostly knew my capacity to push them. Limits were suggestions, not borders. I wore my endurance like a quiet badge.

After the stroke, that language stopped working.

The body no longer warned.

It imposed.

I remember an ordinary moment. A meeting. Familiar faces. A normal exchange. Nothing dramatic. I was listening, nodding at the right time, keeping my expression steady.

Then suddenly a deep fatigue.

Not the kind you manage.

The kind that decides.

My eyes stayed open. My posture stayed polite. My mouth stayed composed. I even said the right words at the right time.

But inside something cracked.

I reread the same email three times and still did not know what it said.

The cursor blinked like it was waiting for a version of me that was not there.

I left that room and the hallway felt longer than it should have. My steps became careful, as if my body were saying, I can do this, but you will not pretend it costs nothing.

My body had lived with violated boundaries for years.

Not through harm. Through loyalty.

After the stroke, limits organized my days.

There were possible days, days when I could teach, meet, think, decide, and still have something left for home.

And there were impossible days, days when the simple act of getting ready in the morning felt like the entire day's work.

There were sustainable conversations, honest and focused and meaningful.

And there were others that cost too much.

At first this distinction humiliated me internally. Not because it reduced my value, but because it dismantled my illusion of mastery. I had built an identity around being the one who could hold more, stay longer, carry heavier loads.

I had to learn something radical.

Limits are not weaknesses to correct.

They are truths to listen to.

The stroke did not only reveal my physical limits. It forced me to revisit my spiritual and emotional ones.

Before, I asked God for strength to exceed.

Now my prayers changed shape.

Lord, show me what I can no longer do, and give me the courage not to pretend.

Limits did not shrink my calling.

They revealed its size.

They made me ask different questions.

What is truly mine to carry?

What belongs to others?

What belongs to God alone?

The answers confronted me.

I had been carrying what was never mine.

The body had drawn a line.

The spirit had to learn to honor it.

SECTION III — THE TRUTH ABOUT FEAR

I did not like imagining that fear had played a role in how I lived. It did not fit the image I carried of myself. I saw myself as disciplined, courageous, resilient.

Fear did not seem to belong in that picture.

Silence exposed fear I had learned to call discipline.

Mine wore an effective mask.

Usefulness.

To be useful.

To be needed.

To be sought after.

I was proud to be the person people called when they needed help, a listening ear, a plan, a bridge.

I called it service.

It was also survival.

But the silence after the stroke forced me to ask another question.

Who am I when I am not required?

That question scared me more than the diagnosis.

The schedule emptied. Action slowed. Fewer people needed me urgently. I had to exist without producing immediately, without solving, without hosting, without organizing.

That confronted me with an older fear than I expected.

The fear of becoming peripheral.

The fear of being loved for what I do more than for who I am.

I saw it in the simplest scenes.

Sitting next to Kristianna on the couch. No program. No urgency. No problem to solve.

Just presence.

The television was on. Neither of us was watching it.

My mind searched for something to offer. A plan. A helpful comment that would justify my place in the room.

And she did not move away from me.

There was another fear that took longer to name.

The fear of speaking my full truth in spaces where my belonging was not guaranteed.

In my role, I knew how to phrase things carefully, how to translate tension into acceptable language, how to reframe hard realities so they could be heard without causing too much disruption.

I knew how to say hard things safely.

I also knew how to hide inside that safety.

After the stroke, every sentence cost more effort. I began to ask myself,

If I am going to spend this much energy speaking, what am I willing to say, and what am I no longer willing to swallow?

Silence stopped letting me lie.

There were truths I had been bending to preserve harmony.

But the body had already told the truth.

When you negotiate yourself for the sake of acceptance, conflict settles into the flesh.

Spiritually, I had to admit that some of what I had called humility was actually fear. Some of what I had called patience was self-silencing.

In the quiet, God did not ask me to become harsh.

He asked me to stop lying with my silence.

Silence made that decision unavoidable.

SECTION IV — THE TRUTH ABOUT RELATIONSHIPS

Illness redraws relationships quietly.

Who leans in.

Who hesitates.

Who waits.

Who disappears.

I began timing my walk so I would meet fewer people.

I learned which hallway corners gave me the least chance of being seen.

In the silence that followed, another layer emerged.

Every relationship has a price.

Illness shows you what it is.

Some relationships depend on your usefulness. When your capacity changes, their proximity changes.

Others remain but do not know how to stand beside someone who now depends more than before.

And then there are those whose love shifts shape without losing depth.

Kristianna belongs to that last category.

At home she carried more than anyone else. My recovery schedules, medications, sleep, fears that rose at night without warning.

But she also carried something less visible.

The responsibility of helping me belong to myself again without making me feel diminished.

Sometimes she would look at me after hearing others speak about belonging and say simply,

You are very good at what you do. I look up to you.

Her words did not inflate me.

They steadied me.

They reminded me that even slowed down, even wounded, I had not lost the substance of who I was.

Belonging in marriage after illness is not automatic.

It is renegotiated.

Not because commitment disappears, but because roles shift.

I was no longer only a husband.

I was also a patient.

She was no longer only my partner.

She was also my anchor.

Beyond home, silence helped me see relationships more clearly.

Not everyone will make the journey with you.

Some relationships survive effort, not truth.

Every healthy relationship can bear the truth of limits.

Those that cannot require revision.

My prayers changed.

I stopped praying for open doors.

I began praying for protected ones.

SECTION V — THE TRUTH ABOUT FAITH

After illness, my faith did not disappear.

It stopped working the way it used to.

Before the stroke my faith was intertwined with movement. I prayed while driving between obligations. I thanked God for open doors and expanding responsibilities.

When the stroke came, faith could no longer be measured by what I could carry.

I was lying in a hospital bed with nothing to contribute but breath.

In the silence, prayer changed shape.

There were days when I asked for nothing.

I simply stayed before God.

No impressive words.

Only presence.

And in that bareness, something simple rose in my spirit.

You have nothing to prove here.

God was not asking me to be strong.

He was asking me to be true.

True about fear.

True about anger.

True about disappointment.

I wrestled with questions I had never dared to name.

Why do faithful people still struggle?

Why do deception and manipulation sometimes appear to prosper?

Life is not fair.

But God is faithful.

Faith stopped helping me cope.

It began helping me stand.

Faith did not bring back the old Radar.

It began to ground the new one.

SECTION VI — THE TRUTH ABOUT MEANING

Before the stroke, meaning felt clear.

Teaching.

Coaching.

Building belonging in institutions.

All of that remains true.

But after illness meaning without limits became dangerous.

The body asked a different question.

At what cost?

I could no longer generate meaning on credit.

Some days the most meaningful thing I could do was take a walk, drink water, and go to bed early.

I used to call that laziness.

Now I called it obedience.

Meaning shifted.

I stopped asking how much I could do.

I started asking what I could sustain.

Does this align with my season?

Does this align with my health?

Does this align with my family?

The silence dismantled my attachment to heroism.

I did not need to be everywhere.

I needed to be faithful.

SECTION VII — THE TRUTH ABOUT IDENTITY AFTER FRACTURE

Identity shifts after a fracture.

Slowly.

Roles that once felt like skin begin to feel like clothing.

Still real. Still important.

But not the whole story.

The stroke brought me to a place where titles meant nothing.

Lying in a hospital bed I was simply a man whose brain had survived a rupture.

No résumé mattered there.

In that place a deeper question surfaced.

Who am I if I can no longer perform?

The silence asked for another foundation.

I want to be known as a man who fears God.

A man who loves his wife and daughter with intention.

A man who honors his parents and stands with his siblings.

A man whose words heal.

Those are not tasks.

They are ways of being.

Identity after fracture is less about rebuilding the old self.

It is about accepting the self that has arrived.

Slower. More grounded. More rooted.

I am not less than I was before.

I am different.

The question is no longer whether I will be the same.

The question is whether I will remain faithful to what the fracture revealed.

SECTION VIII — WHAT SILENCE DEMANDS

Silence is not rest.

It is fidelity.

The danger after crisis is rebuilding too quickly and calling it recovery when it is simply a return to what made you sick.

Silence asked me to stay longer in the in between.

Present.

Engaged.

Unfinished.

It forced decisions.

Saying no when my yes would come from fear or guilt.

Leaving spaces where dignity was repeatedly disregarded.

Protecting time for rest, prayer, writing, and family.

Each decision was quiet.

Each one was fidelity.

Silence also demanded honesty about what I was postponing.

To write.

To speak.

To build a consulting practice.

To give back to young athletes in Cameroon.

Silence left me no room to avoid that truth.

A season will come where calling and life align.

But it must be built on truth.

Silence is not passive.

It is deeply active.

SECTION IX — WHAT SILENCE MAKES POSSIBLE

Silence rearranged me.

Not through one dramatic moment but through a slow accumulation of alignments and honest decisions.

We do not transmit from control.

We transmit from what we have survived without betraying.

Before the stroke I spoke about resilience, conflict, belonging, and healing from the outside.

After the stroke my words began to carry my own weight.

Belonging was no longer a concept for institutions.

It became the ground I stood on in my own life.

Faith was no longer background belief.

It became the way I moved forward.

Silence prepared the ground for becoming whole again.

Not by erasing the fracture.

But by living honestly inside what it revealed.

Silence asks a final question.

Will I become who I was again?

Or will I remain faithful to who I am becoming?

This is where recovery stops being the goal.

Faithfulness becomes the responsibility.

CONCLUSION

When recovery is no longer the question

Recovery removes urgency.

Survival narrows the field.

Silence widens it.

The truths that rose in the silence did not offer a neat conclusion.

They asked me to live differently.

My mission has not disappeared.

It has been refined.

I am still called to build, to illuminate, to help others recognize what they carry.

But I now do so without sacrificing my body, my coherence, or my belonging.

Healing does not require my disappearance.

It requires my presence.

Silence has spoken enough.

Now I listen.

9

RELEARNING PRESENCE

From Absorption to Vocation

I am not writing this chapter to define presence.

I am writing it because I had to learn it again.

For a long time, I believed I was present.

I was there. Available. Engaged. Responsive.

I answered. I listened. I stayed.

And yet something shifted inside me each time.

A quiet heaviness. A muted tension. A fatigue that had not yet learned how to speak.

I did not know how to name what was happening, so I treated it as normal. The price of seriousness. The cost of care. The hidden side of leadership.

It was only after the illness that I understood.

My presence had not been absent.

It had been absorbent.

Silence had already taught me that what we do not name is still carried. When a system cannot hold tension collectively, it often searches for a human nervous system to hold it privately.

This chapter traces that movement. The passage from a presence that absorbs to a presence that inhabits.

Not through withdrawal.

Through accuracy.

Because this book has never been only about a medical event. It has always been about the inner logic that preceded it and the truth it forced into the open.

The fracture came first.

Then the hidden war of recovery. The relational disorientation. The silence that finally began to speak.

What followed was quieter but more decisive.

Presence stopped being the place where unresolved tension settled.

The body stopped being the final site of regulation.

And in that regained alignment, survival loosened its grip enough for a more durable form of faithfulness to appear.

What follows is not a lesson.

It is the record of an inner reconfiguration. Relational, professional, spiritual.

Anchored in the only ground that remained trustworthy. The body as messenger and truth as the cost of remaining whole.

What I did not anticipate was that presence would become my most demanding discipline at work.

After the stroke life did not wait politely for my recovery narrative to complete itself. The school calendar did what calendars do. It filled. Meetings returned. Students laughed in hallways. A crisis appeared in the morning and needed attention by lunch. A rumor moved through a dorm in the evening and required containment.

The work of belonging and conflict did not pause simply because my body had been forced to.

But my body had changed the rules.

Not by giving me a new ideology. By removing an old capacity.

I could still serve. I could still guide. But I could no longer disappear to make the space feel stable.

And so I had to learn presence again.

SECTION I — PRESENCE CONFUSED WITH ABSORPTION

By the afternoon my coffee was always cold.

I rarely remembered taking a sip. Conversations seemed to replace each other in the same chair across from me. Students slowed near the doorway, then circled back. No one scheduled those conversations. They accumulated.

Over time I began to believe presence meant availability.

People trusted me because I responded. They leaned on me because I did not pull back. I answered before finishing my own thoughts. When no one needed me I felt strangely unnecessary.

I became reliable because I stayed.

Gradually this posture stopped being a role. It became a way of being.

To be present meant to be reachable.

To be engaged meant not to close.

To help meant to take it in.

This logic felt right. It was rarely questioned.

Nothing exploded. Words remained careful.

And yet as I walked out of certain conversations something followed me. A quiet pressure in my chest. As if my ribs were holding something down. I stretched my shoulders the way someone stretches after carrying a bag too long.

At the time I called it the normal cost of engagement.

Today I know it was weight.

I would sit alone for a moment and listen for what I felt.

Nothing had a name.

But my body kept it anyway.

A SCENE I CAN STILL FEEL

Before the stroke, before the body forced the truth into the open, I could walk out of a tense conversation and still appear composed. Sometimes even energized. As if conflict itself gave me meaning.

I remember one afternoon in my office at school. The door was half open. Students moved past in the steady hallway current.

A student sat across from me. Shoulders tight. Eyes bright with anger.

The story was familiar.

A comment in class. A laugh that landed wrong.

"They keep saying it wasn't a big deal."

A teacher who meant well. A friend group fractured overnight.

Identity was present in every sentence even when the student did not yet have the language for it.

"So now I'm the one overreacting."

I did what I had always done.

I listened.

I affirmed.

I reframed.

I found language that could lower the temperature without denying the wound. I offered options. Coaching. Mediation. A restorative conversation.

The student left calmer. That was the visible outcome.

But when the door closed behind them my chest tightened for no reason I could explain.

I sat still with my hands on the desk. The pressure did not match the words we had spoken.

It was not fear.

It was not sadness.

It was storage.

As if my body had become the place where the room left what it could not hold together.

I stood up anyway. Continued my day. Walked to the next meeting. Answered the next email. Smiled at the next student.

And carried what remained as if it belonged to the job.

At the time I called that leadership.

Now I call it absorption.

SECTION II — LEADERSHIP SLOWED BY THE BODY

After the illness something stopped.

Not violently.

The body simply stopped cooperating.

I could no longer respond as before. Reactivity was no longer available.

I had to stop.

Breathe.

Feel whether the body could accompany what the mind proposed.

At first, I experienced this as loss.

Loss of fluidity.

Loss of mastery.

Loss of credibility perhaps.

I believed slowing down would weaken leadership. That silence would create instability. That a delayed response would be read as incompetence.

The first time I did not respond immediately I thought I was creating danger.

None came.

The silence held.

I heard the room. The scrape of a chair leg. Someone tapping a pen once and stopping.

For the first time I understood something simple.

What we call urgency is often fear of staying with the unfinished.

Slowness was not withdrawal.

It was precision.

Fatigue became signal.

Tension became information.

The body began resisting before my mind understood why.

In the past it had held. Compensated. Absorbed.

Now it refused.

And that refusal revealed something essential.

Leading did not mean responding quickly.

Leading meant responding truthfully.

SECTION III — PRESENCE WITHOUT ABSORPTION

The room held a sentence neither of us softened.

I felt the urge to fix it rise in my chest and stop there.

The pause felt longer than it was.

Nothing broke.

Before illness, I believed presence meant responsibility for how conversations ended.

Listening meant containing.

Accompanying meant carrying.

If someone left calmer, I felt useful.

If someone left unsettled, I felt I had failed.

I did not yet see the exchange taking place.

What the room could not hold together I stored in myself.

Recovery forced a distinction.

Presence makes room.

Absorption takes on what is not mine.

The first time I stayed without rushing to repair the discomfort was real. My hands wanted to move. My stomach tightened.

But when the conversation ended, I was still myself.

Not emptied.

That moment changed something.

I could stay without absorbing.

I could listen without preparing myself to fix.

I could say something simple.

"I would prefer to continue tomorrow."

The relationship did not collapse.

And my body no longer had to carry what time itself could hold.

SECTION IV — CONFLICT WITHOUT SELF ERASURE

Before illness I entered conflict prepared.

Prepared to listen. Prepared to contain. Prepared to translate.

My training had taught me how to stabilize a room.

It had made me useful.

But it required something I had not yet named.

It required my disappearance.

After illness that posture was no longer available.

Not because I rejected it.

Because the body would not cooperate.

I began noticing signals.

Tightness in the chest.

Anticipated fatigue.

A subtle constriction.

Before I entered conflict with preparation.

Now I entered with attunement.

I had to sense whether I could remain intact in the space.

Not invulnerable.

Intact.

Sometimes I slowed the process. Sometimes I deferred.

The tension became visible.

But it remained where it belonged.

In the relationship.

Not inside my body.

Peace, I discovered, can sometimes be a transfer of weight.

I stopped accepting that transfer.

SECTION V — PRESENCE AS SPIRITUAL DISCIPLINE

For a long time, my faith sustained endurance.

I prayed for strength.

For constancy.

For the ability not to break.

After the stroke faith could no longer function that way.

Not because it disappeared.

Because it could no longer compensate for what the body could not sustain.

Gradually faith stopped fueling endurance.

It began grounding limits.

I no longer prayed to absorb more.

I prayed to remain truthful.

Presence became a spiritual discipline.

Not because it was gentle.

Because it required alignment.

Alignment has a physical feeling.

The breath drops lower.

The shoulders unclench.

The body stops bracing.

Being present now required attention not only to the other person but to what was happening in me while I was with them.

Compassion stopped meaning substitution.

Faithfulness stopped meaning disappearance.

Trusting God took another form.

Doing less without losing myself.

SECTION VI — INTEGRATION IN DAILY LIFE

The changes did not arrive through announcements.

They arrived through ordinary days.

Through what I stopped carrying automatically.

Some relationships became lighter.

Others became more exposed.

What I once absorbed began appearing openly in the relationship itself.

Not every relationship survived the shift.

I grieved that.

But I also noticed something surprising.

I was less central.

And nothing essential collapsed.

My body stopped being the place where everything ended.

It became a place I could live in again.

SECTION VII — THE CLASSROOM

In the third year after the stroke another integration appeared.

I began teaching French I.

Not to prove anything.

Because I missed the classroom.

Teaching has rhythm.

Structure.

Repetition.

The gift of slow learning.

In a beginner language classroom vulnerability is everywhere.

Students fear sounding foolish. Fear correction. Fear being wrong.

Teachers sometimes absorb that anxiety by rescuing.

After illness I no longer had the energy to rescue.

But I could remain present.

My approach became simple.

Repetition.

Permission to err.

Learning through correction.

Mistakes were not interruptions.

They were the place where learning began.

Presence without absorption became a teaching ethic.

A relational ethic.

A way of remaining whole while fully engaged.

SECTION VIII — WHAT MUST END

An email arrived late at night.

The screen lit the room.

I marked it unread and closed the laptop.

Some patterns had shaped my identity for years.

Answering messages during dinner.

Keeping my phone volume on at night.

Replaying conversations while brushing my teeth.

People appreciated it.

So I continued.

Illness ended that confusion.

These were not virtues.

They were ways the system remained stable by borrowing my nervous system.

The first time I said no I apologized twice.

The third time I did not.

Later it felt like obedience.

What had to end was not service.

What had to end was disappearance in the name of service.

The boundary did not shrink vocation.

It made it livable.

SECTION IX — A VOCATION THAT CAN BE LIVED

There are losses that arrive quietly.

Some relationships had been built around the version of me who absorbed everything.

When that posture ended not every relationship could adapt.

I had to accept that some relationships are seasonal.

That does not make them false.

It makes them limited.

Spiritually this grief taught me something decisive.

Faithfulness is offering what is true and sustainable.

What can no longer come with me is not rejected violently.

It is laid down with respect.

And that necessity has not impoverished my life.

It has made vocation more livable.

It has made life more whole.

CONCLUSION

I sat without reaching for my phone and realized nothing required me immediately.

The room remained quiet long enough for me to notice my breathing.

There are ways of serving that look like fullness while arranging a slow disappearance.

Survival taught me to stop living against what within me already knows.

I woke without bracing for the day.

A fragile coherence.

But a real one.

One that no longer proves itself through exhaustion.

Survival, once it has done its work, must be laid down.

Otherwise, it becomes a respectable prison.

What illness made impossible, repeating the same life under the same conditions, made something else possible.

A faithfulness that no longer requires destruction.

A responsibility that no longer demands disappearance.

This chapter does not close a story.

It steadies the ground.

From endurance to coherence.

From usefulness at all costs to responsibility grounded in truth.

Between holding everything and leaving everything a habitable space opens.

It is in that space that I now stand.

Present.

10

SECOND BEGINNING

From Survival to Vocation

I am writing it because I have come to understand that my way of seeking conclusions was often a way of protecting myself. For me, to conclude meant organizing life into something readable, intelligible, transmissible; giving stable form to what had been chaotic; placing a final period in order to breathe.

But what the stroke taught me, and what life afterward confirmed, is that some experiences refuse conclusion without betrayal. They ask for something other than summary. They require sustained fidelity, a way of inhabiting continuity without forcing it to become simple.

For a long time, I believed that healing meant returning.

Returning to a former state.

Returning to a reliable body.

Returning to endurance without questions.

I used the word integration, but part of me was still hoping for restoration: hoping to regain the ability to carry without adjusting, to move forward without listening, to meet expectations without negotiating the cost.

The fracture did not merely interrupt me.

It displaced the center of gravity of my inner life.

It made visible fragile balances I had been compensating for without acknowledging them. It forced my body to speak where I had become skilled at functioning without saying anything.

I understood this before the stroke conceptually.

I understood it afterward bodily.

And then, later, quietly, another beginning arrived. Not to erase what had happened, but to enter into it.

The birth of my daughter did not offer me a blank page.

It offered me a new responsibility within a story already marked.

That is why this chapter is not called New Life.

I did not become innocent again. I became attentive. And that attentiveness is not a weakness. It is a maturity acquired at the cost of the fracture.

Second beginning means something else.

Life begins again with memory, with acknowledged limits, with a demand for truth that no longer tolerates denial.

This chapter is also the place where I must name two presences without whom this continuity would not have been possible: Kristianna, whose patience preceded my clarity, and my daughter, whose very existence made conditional belonging impossible.

I want these pages to offer a livable hope. Not a hope that promises a return to sameness, but one that affirms that a coherent life remains possible after fracture, provided we do not confuse faith with erasure, courage with speed, or love with self-sacrifice.

SECTION I — THE DAY AMARAH ARRIVED

Amarah was born on a Friday during the final week of August, precisely as the school year was beginning.

This detail is not incidental. It says something about the world I inhabit, a world structured by calendars, responsibilities, expectations. Students arriving with their needs and their histories. Colleagues, meetings, urgencies. Rhythms that resume without waiting for inner life to stabilize.

I had long known how to hold that world. I had long been reliable within it.

But the stroke had already shifted something. I could no longer act as if holding were enough. And that Friday, while the outside world was preparing to resume its pace, I was entering a space where pace no longer obeyed the same rules.

The birth had been planned.

We carried this knowledge quietly, like something precious, preparing inwardly rather than announcing it to the world.

We left very early, around five in the morning.

It was still dark. The house felt unusually quiet, as if it were holding its breath.

Kristianna, her mother, and I were there.

Before leaving, we prayed. A simple prayer. No staging. A prayer of dependence, that God would bless the day, that everything would unfold well, that peace would cover what we could not control.

Kristianna was very nervous. She was shaking. She asked the doctors many questions. I watched her body searching for an anchor. And I understood.

I too was carrying a hospital memory, a memory in which medical space is not only a place of care but also a place of truth.

I surprised myself by being more grounded than I expected. Not because I was detached, but because I had learned something simple.

Panic protects nothing.

Panic burns energy without producing safety.

Presence sustains.

I wanted to be a support for Kristianna. And I was already accepting that this support would not consist in solving anything. It would consist in being there.

The drive to Mission Hospital was simple. Registration was quick. An efficiency that was almost reassuring.

But inside, normality had ceased to exist.

We were in a passage.

When they explained to Kristianna's mother that she could not accompany us, that only one person was allowed, I saw Kristianna tense, then soften. They shared a brief but dense moment. An adult daughter becoming a daughter again for a minute. A mother becoming refuge again.

Even when one is strong, one needs a witness.

We were taken to a room. One nurse came. Then another. Instructions. Measurements. Verifications.

Kristianna kept asking questions. She was still shaking.

They gave me medical clothing and special shoes. I changed.

That gesture marked me.

Putting on that uniform meant accepting entry into a space where I was not in control.

Perhaps fatherhood begins there.

Kristianna asked to go to the bathroom. Then again. Then again.

I did not try to reduce her nervousness. I did not offer those automatic phrases meant to soothe without listening. I looked at her. I spoke softly. I let her shake without judging her.

Because dignity sometimes consists simply in not being rushed by one's own need for comfort.

When the nurse returned to take her to the operating room, I felt the silence thicken.

Kristianna left.

I remained alone for about twenty-five minutes.

Not long on a clock.

Very long in a waiting body.

That silence reminded me of the silence that followed the stroke: the silence of not knowing, of not controlling, of having only one option—trust.

This time the silence did not terrify me.

It humbled me.

I prayed without words.

I simply stayed.

When they came to get me, I walked down the corridor toward the operating room.

There were many people. A full team. A precise organization. A speed that was almost disorienting.

A nurse stood near Kristianna's head. A large curtain separated us from the procedure.

I did not look.

The doctor spoke to me, but I do not remember her words.

I mostly remember Kristianna's face. The cold she seemed to feel. That fragile strength that moved me deeply.

Then, in less than five minutes, Amarah was there.

Her cry filled the room.

It crossed the curtain.

It crossed my body.

And I understood something simple.

Life does not negotiate.

It arrives.

The doctor said she was beautiful. A nurse asked me to accompany her while they weighed her.

I saw her already strong, placed on her stomach, her head astonishingly steady.

The nurse smiled. "She is strong."

She asked whether I wanted to hold her.

I said yes.

And as I held her, I felt a joy that did not ask my past to be silent. A joy that erased nothing. A joy that entered a marked life without fear.

I returned to Kristianna.

They placed Amarah on her chest, skin to skin.

Kristianna was crying with relief and gratitude. I watched her breathe differently, not only because the surgery was over, but because her daughter was there.

Later we were taken to recovery, then to the hospital room.

And there I felt a quiet shock.

The room looked like the one where I had been placed after the stroke.

Same configuration.

Same light.

Same hospital spaciousness.

This was not an insignificant coincidence.

Life was bringing me back into a space of fragility, but for a joyful event.

As if to say:

This place is not your trauma.

This place is a passage.

You can live a birth here as you once lived a recovery.

SECTION II — HEALING AFTER BIRTH

We spent two nights in the hospital.

Nurses rotated day and night. Doctors came and went. Everything was monitored. Everything was serious.

And yet, at the heart of this rigor, there was immense tenderness.

The next day we called my parents and my brothers and sisters.

No one had known that Kristianna was pregnant.

In our family and in our culture, certain blessings are carried quietly until they arrive safely in the world. Joy can be vulnerable. Some miracles are protected by silence before they are shared.

Their voices filled the room.

A wave of love.

When we returned home, however, life did not slow down.

Nights were difficult. Crying. Fatigue. Adjustments.

And very quickly we realized that Kristianna's recovery was not unfolding as expected.

Her incision was not closing properly.

What followed were several urgent returns to Mission Hospital.

I was working, coaching football in the afternoons, moving between the field and the hospital. A strange split world where responsibility and vulnerability coexist.

The doctor eventually had to reopen the wound completely.

Seeing that moment was jarring. The body can be fragile even when everything appears calm on the surface.

She suggested that I perform the daily packing of the wound at home.

For the first time in a long time, I refused immediately.

I knew my limits.

I was not trained for that, and I would not pretend competence where I did not have it.

That refusal mattered.

It was one of the first times I refused not from fear, but from respect for limits.

The Wound Care Center at Mission Hospital received us the next day.

The nurses were extraordinarily attentive.

Gentle.

Patient.

Human.

Eventually the doctor proposed a wound vacuum, a device that would support the healing process.

Within days it was installed.

From that point on we returned three times a week for nearly two months.

Slowly, healing resumed.

The machine was inconvenient, but it was doing the work Kristianna's body could not yet complete alone.

By the final weeks, Kristianna was strong enough to drive herself to appointments again.

Watching her regain that independence was quietly powerful.

Life continued.

And it was precisely there that I understood something decisive.

Amarah's birth was not a happy ending placed after the ordeal.

It was an entry.

A demanding entry.

She entered a life already marked.

I did not meet her as a man restored to innocence.

I met her as a man carrying memory.

And yet nothing in her arrival was heavy.

Her beginning did not ask me to forget what my body had endured.

It asked me to remain alive within what was coming.

And that distinction would become decisive.

SECTION III — MEMORY WITHOUT FEAR

For a long time, memory lived in my body as a diffuse tension. It regulated my pace. It introduced caution where I once knew only momentum.

After the stroke that memory became vigilance: monitor, avoid, anticipate, correct.

This vigilance was necessary. It protected me. But it carried a risk. A body that lives in permanent alert does not heal. It tightens.

Amarah's birth shifted that memory.

Not by erasing it, but by giving it direction.

I did not become attentive because I feared dying.

I became attentive because someone was going to learn the world by watching me.

Fear asks, What if it happens again.

Memory asks, How can I remain present long enough to be reliable.

That shift changed everything.

It transformed vigilance into orientation.

Discipline became necessary. Medication. Monitoring. Diet. Choices repeated daily whether I felt strong or not.

One night the house was quiet. I stood in the kitchen with the blood pressure monitor in my hand. I did not want to measure. Not from negligence. From fatigue.

I slid the cuff onto my arm. The machine tightened.

For a moment the memory of the hospital corridor returned. The idea that the body can tip without warning.

I closed my eyes. I breathed.

The number appeared. Not perfect. Not catastrophic. Simply real.

And I understood something essential.

Discipline did not need to be heroic.

It needed to be ordinary.

Like washing your hands.

Like locking the door.

I was not monitoring myself to survive.

I was regulating myself to last.

I also transformed my diet. I eliminated sugar completely. Three years have now passed without it. Not as a symbolic act. As a daily practice.

Faith did not replace discipline.

It sustained it.

After Amarah's birth, this discipline stopped being purely personal.

It became relational.

I am not holding on only for myself.

I am holding on in order to be here.

SECTION IV — UNCONDITIONAL BELONGING

Amarah entered my life without asking me to prove anything.

I did not meet her from a place of finished preparation or recovered solidity. I met her while my body still carried the memory of fracture.

And yet her belonging to me was immediate.

She did not wait for me to be ready.

She did not condition her place on my recovery.

She belonged.

For a long time I believed belonging came from contribution. From usefulness. From reliability. From being necessary enough to justify one's place.

Her presence disarmed that belief.

With her there is no audition.

No negotiation.

I belong because I am here.

She belongs because she exists.

That simplicity is radical.

It revealed the confusion I had carried elsewhere.

I had confused belonging with merit.

Recognition with usefulness.

Faithfulness with self-erasure.

Her dependence requires something different.

Not intensity.

Continuity.

She does not measure reliability by brilliance or speed.

She measures it by return.

What reassures her is that I am there again tomorrow.

That lesson slowly reconfigured everything.

In leadership I stopped trying to intervene spectacularly in moments of crisis. I now seek coherence over time.

In love the lesson is similar. What lasts is not intensity but repeated faithfulness.

And in belonging the change is liberating. I no longer need to make myself indispensable to remain legitimate.

I can belong without negotiating myself.

One night during paternity leave I held her for a long time against my chest. She was restless, insisting softly. I walked slowly across the living room so the floor would not creak.

Eventually she stopped.

Not like a miracle.

Like trust.

Her body relaxed completely.

And in that moment, I understood something about faith.

Faith is sometimes simply staying present long enough for another life to rest.

SECTION V — FAITH AFTER FRACTURE

Amarah's birth did not answer my questions about suffering.

It displaced them.

Faith once helped me interpret events. After the stroke I searched for meaning. Why did this happen? What was God teaching me?

Her arrival made those questions secondary.

Nothing in her birth explained the stroke.

But faith became necessary in a different way.

Not to justify the past.

To sustain the future.

Faith shifted from explanation to gesture.

It now lives less in what I conclude than in what I practice each day:

choosing rest when exhaustion is praised,

protecting health when culture rewards depletion,

remaining present when avoidance would be easier.

Faith is no longer a strategy of protection.

It is a practice of fidelity.

Raising a child makes spiritual illusion impossible.

You cannot hold a new life while pretending everything is under control.

You love within uncertainty.

And faith becomes the courage to remain coherent within that uncertainty.

I pray less that nothing will happen.

I pray more that my life will not contradict what I believe.

Because she will learn long before she understands.

She will feel my rhythm.

My tension.

My calm.

Faith therefore becomes responsible.

Not spectacular.

Not heroic.

Simply coherent.

SECTION VI — CONTINUING WITH RESPONSIBILITY

This second beginning was not given to me as a repair.

It was entrusted to me as a responsibility.

One morning I sat in the car before leaving for work. The engine was running. Messages were waiting. The day was ready to swallow me whole.

Inside the house Amarah was sleeping.

I felt the old logic beginning to assemble again: accelerate, organize, prove, hold.

I placed the phone on the passenger seat.

And I recognized a familiar signal in my chest. Not pain. Not dizziness. Just tension.

You are becoming again what your body has already paid for.

I turned off the engine.

I stayed there for a minute.

That gesture repaired nothing. It simply told the truth.

I am no longer free to pay in silence.

Fatherhood does not add a role to my identity.

It rereads responsibility.

Before, responsibility meant carrying more, holding longer, absorbing without failing.

Today it means carrying rightly: carrying what belongs to me, naming what does not, refusing what compromises duration.

I cannot model exhaustion and call it devotion.

I cannot glorify fatigue and call it love.

What I live becomes a climate.

And that climate becomes a language.

Four months of fatherhood confirmed something simple.

Nothing has stabilized.

But everything has oriented.

I move more slowly.

Not from fear.

From precision.

SECTION VII — THE OPEN ENDING

I no longer want to conclude in order to reassure myself.

Life does not close.

It continues.

Trust today is not a permanent feeling.

It is a repeated choice.

A choice to live in truth before the body is forced to speak.

Unacknowledged tension does not disappear.

It accumulates.

I listen earlier now.

I regulate sooner.

I slow down without guilt.

My life is no longer only my own.

There is a child learning the world through mine.

I do not want love to resemble exhaustion.

I do not want vocation to resemble war against the body.

So I trust limits the way one trusts a fence that protects a home.

Not to imprison.

To preserve.

I also trust truth spoken early.

Not truth that accuses.

Truth that prevents.

To say I am tired.

To say I am accelerating.

To say I need rest.

Not because I am fragile.

Because I am responsible.

Trusting life now means something simpler:

living without illusion,

but also without hardness.

I do not close this story.

I stabilize a direction.

And I name the one who makes that direction irreversible.

Amarah.

I speak her name as a commitment:

to remain present,

to protect continuity,

to honor the body,

to inhabit limits.

The fracture is part of my story.

It must not become my identity.

I do not close the narrative.

I keep the posture.

CONCLUSION

WHAT I PRACTICE WHEN NO ONE IS WATCHING

There is a part of this second beginning that cannot be seen.

It produces no spectacle.

It unfolds in small daily choices.

Most days nothing happens.

There is waking up.

The body assessed without anxiety.

Medication taken without negotiation.

Food chosen with simplicity.

This is where survival becomes practice.

Discipline is not strained willpower.

It is calm fidelity to what I already know.

Some disciplines are not temporary measures.

They are forms of respect.

Respect for the body.

Respect for the life that now depends on my endurance.

When conflict between what I want and what my body can sustain disappears, the organism regulates differently.

The nervous system exits alert mode.

I no longer live reacting to trauma.

I live from integrated knowledge.

And that integration did not happen through understanding.

It happened through repetition.

Right gestures repeated.

Necessary refusals repeated.

This is how the body learns it no longer needs to shout.

TRANSMITTING WITHOUT DISCOURSE

I do not explain blood pressure to my daughter.

And yet she is already learning.

In the rhythm of the house.

In the way I stop.

In the way I return.

Transmission is climatic.

Discipline lived quietly teaches that one can care without tightening, commit without wearing down, endure without sacrificing.

LISTENING BEFORE FRACTURE

I know something now that I did not know before.

The body warns long before it collapses.

Through breath.

Through irritability.

Through fatigue.

Before, I endured these signals.

Today I interrupt them.

Not by panic.

By adjustment.

WHAT REMAINS OPEN

I do not know what the future will hold.

I do not know what limits will still appear.

But I know this.

I am no longer required to wait for collapse to change.

I am no longer required to sacrifice the body in order to serve.

This knowledge is not certainty.

It is orientation.

FINAL OPEN LINE

If this book has a fidelity, it is here.

Not to promise a strength that denies fragility.

Not to propose a healing that erases.

But to make something visible.

A life after fracture is possible.

A disciplined life without hardness.

A faithful life without heroism.

A life that listens early, adjusts often, and continues without lying.

The second beginning is not behind me.

It is in the way I live today.

And in the way I choose, again tomorrow,

to remain present

without illusion,

without flight,

without betraying myself.

And this is how I continue.

EPILOGUE

I end this book where my life continues, not at a finish line, but in a slower way of living.

In the hospital I was not gripped first by fear of death. I was overwhelmed by exhaustion, by how small I suddenly felt, by how fragile my body had become in a room where even the air felt uncertain. I remember lying there, aware that my life could tilt at any moment, and yet too tired to fight the thought. Fatigue, not fear, was the clearest message that day. Fatigue was the body's record of what I had carried without language.

The stroke did not close my story. It slowed me down enough to hear it. I learned that my body is not my enemy and silence is not my protector. I learned that belonging is not something I must buy with quiet sacrifice. It is something I can receive by telling the truth and staying present.

In the beginning I believed peace meant never disturbing the room. Now I know peace can mean naming what hurts and trusting that I will still belong. I no longer stay silent to keep the peace while my body prepares the cost.

Recovery did not bring me back to who I was. It brought me closer to who I am. I move more slowly. I listen sooner. I rest without shame. I speak before my body has to.

Kristianna taught me that love does not rush healing. Amarah reminds me every day that my life is being watched, not judged, but trusted. What a child learns first is not what we believe but how we regulate what we carry. God met me in weakness and stayed with me when I had no strength left to perform.

The body does not protest randomly. It registers what has been held too long without being shared. Fatigue is often the cost of carrying alone what belongs in relationship.

Say what is true. Let belonging be a gift, not a debt.

This book is not a map back to normal. It is a path toward alignment. Living so your body does not need crisis to be heard. Living so your heart can breathe without fear. Living so you can stand in your life without disappearing inside it.

Some nights I stand in the hallway and listen before going to sleep. Her breathing is even, and my chest does not tighten. Nothing needs fixing. That is how I now recognize peace.

I am still walking that path. Some days I walk well. Some days I stumble. Every day I choose again to listen, to stay honest, and to remain open to love.

And tonight, that is enough.

ABOUT THE AUTHOR

Radar Onguetou is a teacher, speaker, Conflict Resolution practitioner, and writer whose work focuses on conflict, belonging, and the quiet ways the body carries what life leaves unresolved. He serves as Director of Community Engagement and Belonging at a private school in North Carolina, where he works with students, educators, and families to build communities where people can live, learn, and speak with dignity.

Radar holds a doctorate in conflict analysis and resolution. His professional life has been shaped by extensive experience listening to people in moments of tension. Students searching for their place. Colleagues navigating disagreement. Communities trying to remain whole while facing difficult truths. Through that work he came to see that conflict is not only something that happens between people. When it is not addressed honestly it often continues inside the person who carries it.

He also speaks and consults with schools and organizations on conflict, belonging, leadership, and the hidden emotional cost of unresolved tension in human systems. His work invites leaders and communities to reflect on how honesty, limits, and care can coexist without sacrificing the well-being of the people who carry responsibility.

In 2023 Radar suffered a stroke while traveling in Cameroon, the country where he was born. That experience changed the way he understood the connection between the body, stress, and the cost of unspoken tension. Recovery became more than a medical process. It became a slow rediscovery of limits, faith, and presence.

This book grows out of that journey. It is both a personal story and a reflection shaped by professional practice. It explores what happens when life interrupts the rhythm we believed was normal and what it means to rebuild a life without denying the fracture that changed it.

Radar writes from the conviction that healing does not erase what has happened. It teaches us how to live truthfully with it. Through his work he invites individuals and institutions to reflect on how belonging, honesty, and care can exist together without sacrificing the body or the soul.

He lives in North Carolina with his wife Kristianna and their daughter Amarah. His life today moves at a slower and more attentive pace. Each day is guided by a simple commitment. To remain present to the people and responsibilities entrusted to him.

www.ingramcontent.com/pod-product-compliance
Lightning Source LLC
La Vergne TN
LVHW050805061126
851857LV00012B/689